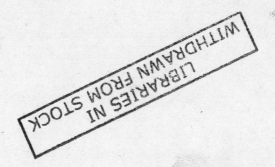
The Girl With Two Lives

The Girl With Two Lives

A Shocking Childhood. A Foster Carer Who Understood.
A Young Girl's Life Forever Changed.

ANGELA HART

bluebird
books for life

First published 2018 by Bluebird
an imprint of Pan Macmillan
20 New Wharf Road, London N1 9RR
Associated companies throughout the world
www.panmacmillan.com

ISBN 978-1-5098-3907-0

1 3 5 7 9 8 6 4 2

A CIP catalogue record for this book is available from the British Library.

Typeset in Utopia Std by Palimpsest Book Production Ltd, Falkirk, Stirlingshire

Printed and bound by CPI Group (UK) Ltd, Croydon CR0 4YY

Visit **www.panmacmillan.com** to read more about all our books
and to buy them. You will also find features, author interviews and
news of any author events, and you can sign up for e-newsletters
so that you're always first to hear about our new releases.

1

'They couldn't cope with her a day longer'

The first thing I saw when I opened the front door was a large cage containing a scampering hamster.

'Oh!' I exclaimed. 'I wasn't expecting that!'

A short, stout girl with a shiny forehead and an untidy cap of black hair was staring at me warily from behind the cage. I could only see the top part of her wide face but it was clear from her expression she wasn't happy, and she certainly wasn't smiling.

'Well I never!' I grinned, trying to break the ice. 'I don't know who to say hello to first!'

I looked from the girl to the hamster, and then to the female social worker who was standing behind them. The social worker gave me a friendly smile and said hello but the girl continued to stare at me suspiciously. The hamster stopped scampering for a moment and pressed its twitching nose up to the bars of the cage to have a long, hard look at me. Its eyes were very dark and marble-like – small versions of the girl's, in fact – and for a moment I felt rather intimidated at having two sets of watchful eyes trained on me like this.

I took a breath and reminded myself of one of the many truths I had learned about fostering over the years: however you feel as a foster carer, it is always much more difficult for the child than it is for you, especially at the very start of a placement.

'Come on in, Danielle. What is your hamster's name?'

Danielle didn't reply and didn't move and her social worker, Susan, helpfully offered the name Scooter.

'What a great name!' I said. 'I like that. We've been looking forward to you arriving, Danielle, and it's very nice to meet you and Scooter, and you, Susan. Can I help carry the cage?'

Danielle shook her head very slightly. She seemed a bit confused, which is often the case when a child arrives at our door.

'It's OK. I like having pets around the house. Do come on in!'

Encouraged by Susan, Danielle slowly stepped into the house, wrapping her arms even more tightly around the cage as she did so. Now I could see that she was not just stout; Danielle was extremely large for a twelve-year-old girl, and she caught her elbows on the doorframe as she bundled herself and Scooter into the hallway. I led the way through to the kitchen, where Danielle looked shiftily around the room before tentatively placing the cage on one end of the table. When I invited her to sit down she perched herself awkwardly on the chair closest to the cage, crossing her arms in front of her and hunching her shoulders forward, as if to hide as much of her body as she could.

I didn't know very much at all about Danielle at this stage. As well as being passed by Social Services to take in foster children of all ages, my husband, Jonathan, and I are specially trained to look after teenagers with problems that make it difficult for them to live with mainstream foster carers. We had many years of experience and had encountered all sorts of specialist needs over the years, but of course each child brought a unique set of issues. We didn't know what Danielle had difficulties with yet, but this was not unusual. Nor was it out of the ordinary for us to be asked to take in a child with specialist needs who was not yet a teenager: it was, and still is, a case of getting children who are in care into the best possible foster home available at the time, as quickly as possible.

I'd received an initial phone call from our support social worker, Nelson, earlier that week, asking if we could potentially take Danielle in for a short period of respite care.

'Her foster family is struggling and need a break,' he had said. 'I'll get more details as soon as I can. Would you be willing to have her stay this weekend, Friday through to Sunday night?'

'That's fine,' I said after quickly checking with Jonathan. 'We'll be happy to have her.'

We had been fostering for twenty years at that time. Despite only being asked to take Danielle in for the weekend, Jonathan and I were well aware that respite care could extend beyond the short period Social Services hoped it would cover. We were very used to that and didn't mind the uncertainty, and that is still the case today.

On many occasions we've taken in a child for one weekend and they have subsequently come to us for respite care every weekend for many months or even longer, and some have ended up moving in full-time.

Our previous placement – a child of sixteen who had been with us as a 'stepping stone' for a few weeks whilst awaiting a flat of her own – had moved out just days earlier. It was highly unusual for us to have no children at all under our roof, and, before Nelson called, Jonathan and I had been toying with the idea of going away for a few days.

'There goes our mini-break!' Jonathan had grinned after Nelson's call.

I didn't even have to ask if Jonathan was being serious, because he and I very rarely refuse to take in a child. We only ever say no if we feel we genuinely can't help, or if we don't think the child will fit in with those already in placement. Once, a child came for an introductory visit while we already had two other children living with us. The atmosphere was very tense in the house for the whole time she was staying, and we decided it would not be beneficial to the others to agree to have her move in permanently. Our instincts proved to be right: when she left, the other kids breathed a sigh of relief and told us that the girl had been spitting on them and bullying them behind our backs.

In all the years we've been fostering we have never had a holiday away on our own together, but this has not bothered us. The weekend breaks, caravan trips and holi-days abroad we often have with the children are always really good fun – well, nearly always! And we also have our flower shop to consider. We've been running the family business throughout all the time we've been fostering, ever since we took it over from my mum in the eighties. The shop is attached to our town house and is in a parade on the fringes of the town, which is very convenient. Our assis-tant and friend Barbara has been with us for a long time and is very flexible and willing to do overtime whenever we need cover. To this day she is forever telling us she'll 'hold the fort' if the two of us ever need to get away for an extra break on our own, but the truth is we rarely have the oppor-tunity and we still find it impossible to say no when we know a child needs a home.

'There'll be plenty of chances for weekend breaks in the future,' I had said after Nelson called, and Jonathan gave me a knowing smile and said he couldn't agree more.

Even after two decades of non-stop fostering, and with both of us in our fifties, we still felt a familiar, positive wave of anticipation whenever a new placement was discussed. We thrived on the challenge of taking in another child, whatever problems they may have, just as we still do today.

By the time Nelson called again a couple of days later it was mid-morning on a weekday and Danielle was now on the emergency list, as her placement had broken down.

'She's on her way to the office with her social worker, Susan, and all of her belongings,' Nelson had explained.

'She was excluded from school yesterday and her foster carers – or should I say former foster carers – said they couldn't cope with her a day longer. The fact we were in the process of arranging respite care didn't help. They had had enough, unfortunately. Now Danielle needs an emergency placement.'

Social Services generally try to avoid taking a child to an office like this, but sadly it happens from time to time, when there is really no other option. Jonathan and I agreed that Danielle could come to us within the hour. The fact Nelson had said that Danielle's former foster carers had 'had enough' was concerning, but certainly did not put us off in any way. The very idea that a child of twelve was without a place to call home was very upsetting, and we both wanted to help as much as we possibly could.

People have often asked us how we can take on children we know virtually nothing about, other than the fact they have 'issues' and need specialist help.

'Whatever problems we might be inviting into our own home, we'll never be in as bad a place as a child needing a foster home, and particularly one who is on an emergency list,' I have said many times. 'You have to be optimistic. You have to think what you can offer the child, not what may go wrong and how they might affect you.'

Those words flickered through my head now, as I looked at Danielle sitting at our kitchen table. Jonathan was introducing himself to her politely and she was giving him a steely stare and saying nothing. The hamster cage was emitting an unpleasant smell of stale, damp straw, and as I stepped towards her and asked Danielle if she'd like a drink I realised she didn't smell very good either. There was a noticeable odour of urine and stale sweat surrounding her and I could see that her hair was in need of a good wash. Her clothes were grubby and didn't fit properly, and she had what looked like yesterday's black eyeliner smudged under her eyes.

You need to be optimistic, Angela. You have to think what you can offer the child.

Jonathan busied himself with putting the kettle on as he asked Danielle what her hamster was called. He got no reply at all and Susan intervened, saying, 'Danielle, shall I tell Jonathan the name of your hamster?'

When no reply came again Jonathan cheerfully said that he didn't want to be told the name.

'Let me guess,' he said playfully. 'Is it a boy or a girl?'

He paused then filled the silence.

'He looks like a boy. Is it Norris? Or Barry?'

Danielle didn't crack her face.

'Oh, I've got it! Of course! His name is Justin Timberlake, isn't it?'

Danielle rolled her eyes and gave a little snort, but at least it was a reaction, and Jonathan immediately started asking her whether she liked Justin Timberlake, and if not, then what music did she like?

'I like Robbie,' she mumbled eventually, very reluctantly.

'Oh, a Robbie Williams fan? Angela likes him too. I think

7

if you're lucky I might be able to find some Take That CDs. I think they might be in the car . . .'

As Jonathan tried his best to keep the one-sided conversation going, Susan took me to one side to give me the standard paperwork handed over whenever we take in a child on respite care. This generally contains emergency contact numbers and some basic details about the child, such as their date of birth and the type of care order they have in place. Danielle was under a full care order, which meant Social Services had overall responsibility for her, and Susan explained she had been in care since she was five years old. The foster carers whose home she had just left were meant to be her 'forever family', meaning the plan had been that Danielle would stay with them until she was at least sixteen and ready to live more independently.

'Danielle moved in with her forever family at the start of the last school holidays,' Susan said. A quick calculation told me Danielle had been with the family for less than two months. 'She went back to school this week but was excluded yesterday morning,' Susan continued. 'The family say the last twenty-four hours have been impossible and they simply can't keep her any longer. I'm afraid I don't know the details of her exclusion as yet.' She then explained that Danielle was at a school for children with specialist needs.

'The priority is to find another suitable school that will take her. At the moment I have no idea where that will be, so of course I can't tell you how long we'll need you to have her staying with you.'

'It's fine,' I said, glancing over at Danielle and Jonathan, who were both peering into Scooter's cage and talking about what kind of food he liked to eat. 'We're used to that, of course. We'll wait to hear more from you, Susan.'

'Thanks, Angela. I'll be in touch as soon as possible, and good luck. I don't know what we'd have done if you hadn't agreed to have her at such short notice. I really am very grateful, and I have to say I admire you both.'

The compliment took me by surprise and I felt a little embarrassed.

'Thanks, and it's just as well I'm not allergic to hamsters!' I joked, as it was the first reply that came into my head.

I said this a little louder than I planned, and just at a point where Jonathan and Danielle had fallen silent. They both looked up and, much to my delight, Danielle smiled at me, albeit ever so slightly.

2

'I didn't mean to do that'

Once her social worker had gone and I'd shown Danielle the bedroom she'd be staying in while she was with us, she asked if she could put Scooter in her room and then have something to eat.

'Of course, sweetheart. Shall we clean out his cage first? And how about a piece of fruit?'

'Can we do the cage later? I'm starving. I didn't have any breakfast. Can I have a bowl of cereal?'

I agreed that she could have a small bowlful, so it wouldn't ruin her lunch, and told Danielle that she could choose from the selection in the cupboard. It's often a good idea to invite a child to help themselves, as it makes them feel more at home and less like a temporary visitor. She seemed happy with this, and after insisting on taking Scooter up to her room she looked through the cupboard containing the cereals.

'You've got a lot to choose from,' she said, taking her time and examining every packet very carefully. I got the impression she was feeling nervous and a bit awkward, which was understandable and perfectly normal.

'I like cereal,' I told her. 'I'm trying to lose some weight and I think it helps if I have a good breakfast. Stops me snacking on biscuits before lunch.'

Danielle suddenly fixed me with a stare. 'Does your husband like you more when you're thinner?'

'Goodness me!' I smiled.

I didn't want to get involved in a conversation along these lines with a twelve-year-old girl I'd only just met. In a jokey voice I said, 'We've been married for more than thirty years and I think it's safe to say that Jonathan doesn't really mind – or notice!'

'I wish I looked like . . . her!' Danielle said.

'Who?'

'Her!'

She had turned to face the middle of the kitchen and was pointing into thin air.

'Who are you talking about, sweetheart?'

Danielle looked dazed and disorientated. I thought she must have been feeling more stressed and anxious than I'd realised, but then she grabbed one of my low-fat cereals from the cupboard and hastily pointed to a tall, slim lady in a red bikini.

'Oh, *her*. I'd like to look like that lady too,' I said. 'Do you think if I eat enough of that cereal I will transform into her, like magic?'

I gave a little laugh and Danielle joined in.

'Actually, I'll have this one,' she said, pulling a different box of cereal out of the cupboard.

I gave her a small bowl and a spoon, fetched a jug of milk from the fridge and set it down on the table.

'Can I have sugar?'

I paused for a split second, wondering if I should tell her that we always liked to say 'please' and 'thank you', but before I could decide if this was the appropriate time or not, she added, 'Please?' herself, very politely.

'Of course. And thank you for asking so nicely. Here's the sugar dispenser. It comes out quite fast, so just be careful.'

'Thank you. I will.'

With that I set about tidying the kitchen worktops, though there really wasn't much to do. I just thought it might be better if I pottered around rather than sitting at the table with Danielle, which might make her feel uncomfortable as I wasn't eating anything.

She filled her bowl, poured on the milk and then I spotted her giving me a little sideways glance, as if checking to see if I was looking at her or not. I glanced away and started sifting through a stack of junk mail that had gathered in the corner of the kitchen, by the door leading to the hall.

'Would you like to bring Scooter back down here?' I asked. 'I think he'd like to have a nice clean cage, so we could sort that out after you've eaten your cereal?'

It can be quite tricky at first, making conversation with any new child who comes to stay. You can't ask anything remotely personal about their family or previous home or life in case it might upset them, trigger bad memories or provoke them to say something they weren't ready to say. In Danielle's case I didn't want to ask about school either, given that she'd been expelled and it was clear from what her social worker had said that the full facts about what had gone on were still being investigated.

'Oops!' Danielle said suddenly, in a slightly over-exaggerated tone.

I turned my head just as her bowl of cereal went crashing to the floor. It smashed on the tiles, splattering milk and soggy pieces of cereal everywhere.

'Oooh, sorry,' she said. 'I didn't *mean* to do that.'

'Never mind,' I said. 'Don't worry.'

'Have I annoyed you? Are you cross with me?'

'No, sweetheart. Accidents happen. Just stay on the chair as you don't have shoes on and I don't want you cutting your feet.'

Danielle did as I asked and watched me intently as I swapped my slippers for shoes, and fetched a dustpan and brush as well as a mop and bucket. As I cleaned up the mess it crossed my mind that there was something not quite right about what had happened. Danielle had sounded insincere when she said she didn't mean to do it, and now she had a strange little smirk on her face. It seemed to me this was not a pure accident, and I wondered if she had done this on purpose, to test me out and see how I would respond. Maybe she wanted me to react angrily, so she had something to complain about to Social Services? I'd come across that scenario on several occasions in the past, when children were still coming to terms with leaving their last carers, wanted to go back to them and were looking for a way out of their new situation.

When the mess was cleared up I fetched Danielle another bowl of cereal, and after she'd finished eating it I showed her where the dishwasher was.

'We always rinse the plates and bowls and so on before stacking them in the dishwasher,' I explained. 'I'll do it for you today. While I do that, do you think you could put the dustpan and brush and the mop and bucket back in the utility room for me?'

I took her bowl and spoon off the table and began to rinse them in the sink, but Danielle didn't budge and just stared at the cloudy water in the mop bucket.

'Why?'

'Because I don't want them in the kitchen. Someone may trip over them and I've finished with them now.'

'Why don't you just put them in the corner, over there?

She nodded to one corner of the kitchen, which was right next to the utility room.

'I could do that, but can you put them in the utility room please, just through the door, there?'

'OK. I'll do it later. I'm busy now. I have to clean Scooter's cage and you've held me up, talking to me so much.'

With that she stood up and went upstairs, leaving me feeling dumbfounded. What a lot of fuss had been created, just by Danielle having a bowl of cereal!

*

I discussed what happened with Jonathan while Danielle was still up in her room, and told him I suspected she was trying to press my buttons, perhaps to give her an excuse to kick out at the situation she was in.

'You could be right,' he said. 'It wouldn't be the first time a child has tried that tactic. It's understandable, I suppose. Anything is possible. It's good to hear what you're thinking, Angela.'

It may seem that I was overanalysing the situation, but when you've been a foster carer for as long as we have you can't help but think this way and explore all possibilities. Jonathan has very sharp instincts, probably more so than me, and he is a firm believer that you should listen to your gut feeling. He thought for a moment and added, 'If you ask me, I'd say that the most likely explanation is that she's feeling like a fish out of water and was simply testing you. Naturally, Danielle wants to know where she is with you. Perhaps she wants reassurance that you're not going to fly off the handle if she makes a mess?'

'That's probably it,' I said thoughtfully. 'We could do with finding out why she first went into foster care when she was so little. She was five, wasn't she?'

Jonathan nodded. 'Yes. And it would be helpful to know why she was expelled from school and why she is under a full care order. I wonder what the situation is with her parents?'

'Quite.'

We were thinking like this because we knew that if she

15

had no school place, the likelihood was that Danielle would be staying with us for longer than just a few days.

The fact Danielle was under a full care order most likely meant that her birth parents were either unfit or unavailable, for whatever reason, to care for their daughter, leading to her being taken off them by Social Services. It's not unusual to have precious little information at the start of a respite placement, however, and Jonathan and I looked forward to hearing more.

Later on I showed Danielle how to use the shower and told her where we kept the towels she could help herself to.

'Your dirty laundry can go in the basket by the door in your bedroom,' I explained. 'I'm putting the washing machine on in the morning, if you have anything you'd like me to wash?'

We were standing on the landing outside her bedroom when I said this. A little earlier Danielle had taken Scooter downstairs to clean out his cage then gone back upstairs. Then she spent about half an hour alone in her room, telling me she wanted to unpack on her own and have some 'quiet time' with her pet.

Now she gave me a somewhat shifty sideways glance as she said, 'Yes please, can you wash a few things for me? Come on, I'll get them for you.'

Danielle led me into her room and I was taken aback by what I saw. There were dirty clothes strewn all over the place, books pulled off the shelf and scattered on the floor and the duvet was in a heap in one corner of the room. The bedside lamp was on its side and a neat pile of coat hangers I'd left beside the wardrobe had been dumped on the dressing table, knocking over a couple of little trinket boxes.

Before Danielle had arrived I'd made sure the room was spick and span, as I always do. She had the biggest of our spare bedrooms on the top floor of our town house and I'd made the bed up with a pretty lime-coloured duvet set that matched the wallpaper and curtains. There was a new box of tissues on the dressing table, all the furniture was polished, the mirrors were shining and I'd aired the room so it smelled nice and fresh.

I always enjoy making up the rooms before any child arrives. Often I get comments about how lovely our house is, or how the bedrooms are 'better than a hotel'. Danielle herself had commented that it was a 'wicked' room when I'd first shown it to her, and this had made me smile. It wasn't that I was particularly house-proud; I wanted everything to be just so because I knew it would make Danielle feel as welcome and comfortable as possible. I think it's the least I can do for the children who stay, knowing that they are probably feeling very strange and unsettled after being taken into care or moved from another foster home.

'Goodness!' I said to Danielle as my eyes scanned the room. Even though I was a bit shocked I tried to keep my tone of voice calm, as I didn't want to upset Danielle in any way. 'Do you need some help here, sweetheart?'

'What do you mean?' she said, jutting out her chin and giving me a defiant look.

'What I mean is, it was tidy in here a short time ago and

now it's not. Can I give you a hand to tidy it up? I could show you the best place to put everything.'

Danielle shrugged. 'Are you angry?'

'No, sweetheart. Everything is new to you. You need time to settle in, and I can help you.'

'So you're not cross?'

'No. It won't take long to tidy up. Do you want to find the clothes you want washing and I'll make the bed, for a start?'

Danielle huffed and puffed as she scooped up her dirty clothes and piled them in the laundry basket.

'Did you have a look at the books?' I asked as I slotted them back onto the bookshelf.

Danielle ignored me.

'Were there any you liked the look of? If not, we have plenty more. I like reading and I've collected lots of books over the years. We have a few other bookshelves around the house. I'll show you later, if you like.'

Danielle scowled and refused to answer me so I carried on tidying up in silence. When the room was back to normal I told her I'd take the washing down to the utility room and explained that after dinner that evening we could watch some television together if she liked.

'Are there any foods you don't eat?'

There was no reply.

'Is there a particular programme you like to watch on TV?'

Still there was no reply.

'OK, well we're having pork chops and mashed potato

18

tonight and, if you fancy joining me, later on I'll be watching some of my favourite soaps that I've recorded.'

'What are we having for lunch?'

'Soup and sandwiches. There's plenty to choose from for the fillings. You can help me make them if you like. Do you like chicken soup? What do you like in a sandwich?'

Again, Danielle completely ignored me.

I went down the first flight of stairs and left the washing on the landing near my bedroom on the first floor of the house while I nipped to the toilet. The moment I locked the door I heard footsteps and then a tap on the door.

'Why?' Danielle asked.

'Pardon? Just a minute, I'm in the loo. I'll be out in a moment.'

'Why did she say that?' Danielle said.

'Hang on, give me a second . . .'

'Why can't I go back?'

'Go back?'

I washed my hands and rushed out as quickly as I could.

'Right, I'm here now. What did you say? What did you want to talk about?'

'I don't.'

'Did you say, "Why can't I go back?"'

Danielle looked at the floor.

'He's out,' she said.

'Who's out?' I asked.

'Scooter.'

'Scooter? What do you mean? Is he out of his cage?'

19

'Yes. The door must have come open by accident and I can't find him. Will you help me look for him?'

'Yes, sweetheart. Oh dear, do you think he's in your bedroom or could he have escaped from there?'

'No idea,' Danielle said, giving me what appeared to be a slightly mischievous smile.

'Right. We'd better start looking on the top floor then, hadn't we?'

'Yes. Are you angry, Alison?'

'No, Danielle. And my name is Angela, remember?'

'Angela, whatever,' she said rudely. 'How come you're not annoyed?'

'Danielle, you said it must have been an accident, and as I said to you earlier when the breakfast bowl fell on the floor, accidents happen, don't they?'

She looked very dissatisfied with this answer.

'I bet you'll tell my social worker I let him out on purpose!'

'No, I will not say any such thing, because that is not what you told me has happened. Scooter seems to have escaped from his cage by accident, hasn't he? That's what you told me, and why would I not believe you? Now, let's stop talking about it and go and find him, shall we?'

Danielle let out a deep sigh. 'Suppose so,' she said. 'And when we've found him, can we go back to my forever family?'

I gave her a kind smile and my heart went out to her. I explained that she was staying with us until Social Services decided what was happening next, but that it was not my understanding that she would go back to her forever family.

I had to be as honest as I possibly could, as I didn't want her to have any false hopes.

Danielle tut-tutted and put her hands on her hips as she told me sternly, 'I'm not happy, you know, An-ge-la.' She exaggerated the pronunciation of my name and this time it seemed very clear she was trying to provoke a reaction in me, perhaps one that would give her the excuse she wanted to ask Social Services if she could go back to her former foster home. I found this very sad. The placement had broken down and Danielle's social worker, Susan, had told me that Social Services were looking for a new school for her, and of course she would need to live near to her school. As Susan had explained, we had no idea where this would be, but as Danielle needed to go somewhere that catered for children who had been excluded from other schools I knew this could mean moving many miles away, as those types of schools were not very common and often over-subscribed. I knew Danielle had had this explained to her too by Susan, but she was obviously finding it hard to accept.

'She's lost and confused, and I think her default response is to try to create trouble,' I said to Jonathan that night.

All day, nothing had been easy. Danielle 'accidentally' dropped her sandwich on the floor at lunchtime and trod on it, and when we had our dinner she tipped the apple sauce out of the jar by turning it upside down over her plate, instead of using the spoon provided.

'Oops,' she said, looking at the huge pile of apple sauce splattered all over her food. 'I can't eat that now, can I?'

21

'Let's hope it's just teething trouble and she starts to settle in tomorrow,' Jonathan said. 'I'm sure things can only get better!'

We were both exhausted. We'd hunted all over the house and found no sign of Scooter, and after dinner Danielle had refused to sit with us in the lounge and messed her bedroom up all over again as she supposedly hunted for her pet.

'I hope you're right, Jonathan,' I said. 'But somehow I can't say I feel optimistic.'

The last thing Danielle had said to me when I went to say goodnight was, 'There must be something that annoys you, Angela. Will you tell me what it is or do I have to keep looking for it?'

She said it in a cheeky rather than a menacing way and I tried to laugh her comment off, but it wasn't really funny. The truth is, I fell asleep that night fretting about what Danielle was going to do next, and feeling impatient to know more about her history so I could do my best to help her enjoy her time with us, rather than seeking to spoil it.

3

'He might get a knife and stab you!'

Danielle came down to breakfast looking cross and upset.

'Can I see my forever family again when I'm grown up?' she asked accusingly.

She was biting her nails and started walking around the kitchen, randomly opening and closing cupboard doors like a much younger child might do. She was also asking nonsense questions and changing the subject so frequently I couldn't keep up.

'Would you rather be a cupboard door or a fridge door, Angela? Or what about a cage door?'

'Oh, now that's a question I've never considered before! I don't know. What about you?'

'None. A car door. And I'd say no children in the car!'

'Why's that Danielle?'

'Have you seen Scooter? Do you think he ate the soap and is being sick somewhere?'

'No. I don't think so . . .'

'Scooter! Scooter! Are you eating the cornflakes, Scooter?'

She peered in the cupboard containing the cereals and looked behind all the boxes. 'Angela, what do you think? Can I see my forever family again when I'm grown up?'

'Sweetheart, I know you must be missing your forever family, and I'm sorry about that.'

'No you're not! You get money for having me, so you're glad I'm here instead of there!'

I took a deep breath. This is an accusation Jonathan and I have had thrown at us several times over the years, one way or another. Lots of children, as well as some parents and extended families, have tried to use the fact we are paid to work as foster carers as a weapon against us. We are paid, of course, but it's not a fortune and, as I've said many times, if money was what motivated us we certainly would not have chosen to be foster carers for all these years.

Unfortunately, in a minority of cases, it seems to be easier for some parents to attack us than it is to face the upsetting reality that they are unable to care for their own children, for whatever reason that may be. Understandably, it's difficult for parents whose children are in care to see Jonathan and I taking over their parenting role, and the distress they feel at the situation occasionally turns to anger that is vented on us. It took me years not to take this personally. Happily this is not the norm: it's far more common for parents to be grateful their child is being looked after in care. However, that doesn't stop the children making accusations of this nature, as Danielle was doing now.

'Would you like to go for a walk into town this morning?'

I asked her, deciding it was best to try to steer the conversation away from the subject of money and her forever family.

'Why?'

'Just to get a bit of fresh air. It's not good to be cooped up in the house all day.'

'What about Scooter? Had you forgotten he was lost or something? We can't leave him on his own, can we? What if he comes out from his hiding place, looking for us?'

'I had an idea about that,' I said. 'Before we go for our walk, why don't we put some carrots out for him, in the corner of the kitchen, and we'll wait to see if he comes out to nibble them?'

I was very pleased to see Danielle's face suddenly light up and she started clapping her hands together excitedly. Once again I thought how much younger she acted than her years. She then started opening and shutting all the kitchen cupboards again, as well as the fridge and even the freezer.

'Where are the carrots?' she demanded. 'Get the carrots, An-ge-la!'

'Can you ask nicely, and put the word "please" on the end of your sentence, Danielle?'

'You didn't! How can you expect me to?'

'Can you ask nicely, and put the word "please" on the end of your sentence, Danielle, *please*?' I repeated, refusing to be rattled by her cheekiness.

'Get the carrots, An-ge-la, pleeease.'

Her tone was still quite rude but I decided not to push

it. I think I'd made my point and I didn't want to antagonise her. Instead I took a large carrot out of the vegetable drawer at the bottom of the fridge, gave it a wash and set about chopping it into small batons. I normally encourage children to help with jobs like this, but something stopped me. I had a little warning bell going off in my head, and I realised that, because of her unpredictable nature and her tendency to lapse into childish behaviour, I just didn't trust Danielle to handle a knife safely, despite the fact she was twelve and should have been more than capable of doing so. It seemed sensible for me to do the job myself, with the least sharp knife I could manage with.

'That knife isn't sharp enough,' Danielle said, watching me hacking the carrot with it rather awkwardly.

She was standing right next to me, so close that I had to tuck in my elbows so as not to bash into her.

'Oh, it'll do! I don't think Scooter will mind if the carrots aren't cut to a professional standard!'

'He might. He might get a knife and stab you!'

I gave an uncertain little laugh and told Danielle she had a very lively imagination. I also asked her to give me a bit of space, as she was standing so close to me it was making me feel uncomfortable.

'I can't imagine Scooter would do such a thing,' I smiled.

'I can.'

Danielle poked my arm as she spoke and I told her there was no need to do that as she had my attention, and it was rude to jab someone like that.

'OK, whatever,' she said, suddenly sounding wistful. She

then began staring at an empty space in the corner of the kitchen.

'Is that where you think we should put the carrots?' I asked.

'What?'

'The carrots?'

'Oh yes. Put them there – all of them! What are you waiting for?'

I chose to ignore her bossiness and stacked up the batons. Then I suggested to Danielle that we could sit very quietly at the table and have a snack and drink while watching and waiting to see if Scooter appeared. She agreed, though she seemed to find it impossible to stay quiet.

'Is there such a thing as hot?' she asked as I made her a drink of hot chocolate and put some biscuits on the table. 'Or is it just cold with hot added? Or is cold just hot with hot taken away?'

'Those are interesting questions,' I whispered. 'You should ask Jonathan as he loves to talk about clever science things like that.'

There was something so childlike about Danielle I found myself talking to her in a way I would to a much younger child. She seemed to respond, and after her rather alarming comment about Scooter stabbing me with a knife I found it endearing and comforting to hear her lapse into such innocent chatter, even if I was trying to get her to have some quiet time.

'Do hamsters like mice?'

'Probably. They're all rodents.'

After I'd answered a stream of other questions – not all of them logical or in any way related to what we were talking about – I suggested we should try to be 'as quiet as mice' for a couple of minutes.

'Let's try two minutes of silence, shall we? Here, I'll set the kitchen timer. Are you ready?'

'What's a rodent?'

'It's the name of the family of little creatures that mice and hamsters belong to. OK, I'm starting the clock!'

Danielle pushed her lips tightly together and nodded. She managed not to talk but then made loud slurping noises whenever she took a sip of her hot chocolate. The liquid dripped down her chin but she appeared not to notice and carried on drinking noisily, drenching her chin more with each gurgling slurp.

Danielle took full advantage of the fact I was not going to speak for two minutes to help herself to more biscuits than I would normally have allowed. I smiled at her and took an extra one myself, and we sat there in companionable silence for the two minutes, enjoying munching on our biscuits as we peered at the pile of carrots on the floor and kept an eye on the door.

Of course, I hadn't really expected Scooter would arrive on cue to nibble the carrots, but I wanted Danielle to know I cared and that I was making an effort to find him. In reality I knew that missing hamsters were sometimes never seen again, at least not alive, in any case. On one memorable occasion, we found a hamster that had been missing for over a week curled up at the bottom of a very tall vase.

He'd obviously fallen in and been unable to escape, and the poor little thing had become dehydrated and perished. I hadn't had any reason to use the vase that week, although I'd dusted the outside of it and hadn't noticed a thing. It was only when a friend visited with her dog that we discovered the dead pet, as the dog immediately sniffed the hamster out and began poking his nose so deeply into the vase that it almost got stuck. We reckoned the hamster must have climbed up the curtains and fallen off, into the vase. It was the only explanation, and it was such a shame.

When the timer pinged Danielle jumped to her feet and said, 'Never mind. Let's go out! Maybe Scooter will come out of his hiding place when we've gone.'

'Good thinking,' I said. 'I love a nice walk into town, don't you?'

'Only when it's not cold. I don't like being cold.'

As well as making a mess and a noise with the hot chocolate, I was dismayed to see that Danielle had eaten the biscuits in quite a revolting way, with her mouth open, like a toddler might. She had crumbs all around her mouth and so I gave her a piece of kitchen roll so she could clean herself up before we went out. I also suggested, gently, that next time she should try to eat more quietly and neatly, with her mouth closed. I didn't want to embarrass her or get her back up, but I did need to teach Danielle how to eat and drink politely. I knew she could do it, as she'd managed it the day before, and perhaps she just needed reminding.

Danielle did as I asked and wiped her face, but not very willingly.

'Is that good enough for you?' she asked in a confrontational tone.

'Yes, that will do. Look! The sun's out now. Let's get going. We'll have a lovely stroll into town.'

Danielle was already heading to the hallway, but as she crossed the kitchen I couldn't help but notice she had a large wet patch on the back of her cream-coloured, knee-length skirt. The patch must have been six inches wide at least, and was very visible on the wide expanse of pleated fabric that hung from Danielle's broad hips.

'Oh,' I said casually. 'You seem to have had an accident, sweetheart. Would you like to go and have a quick shower and put some clean clothes on before we go out?'

'No. I didn't have an accident. It was YOUR fault. You said we couldn't talk for two minutes so HOW could I ask to go to the toilet?'

I was taken aback by Danielle's response but I tried not to show it.

'I think you should clean yourself up,' I said, sticking to my guns. 'You don't want to go to town like that, do you?'

'I don't mind. It's fine. Come on!'

'Danielle,' I said calmly but emphatically, 'you really need to change that skirt and make sure you're dry and smell fresh before we go out.'

I was standing right next to her now, and I could smell the urine.

'No,' she said defiantly. 'You can't make me. But it's fine if you don't want to come to town with me. I can go myself, see if I care!'

I stopped myself being drawn into an argument, and instead found myself saying, 'Fine. Don't go for a shower then.'

It was an instinctive reaction I had, after seeing the defiant look in Danielle's eyes.

'I WILL have a shower,' she announced. 'And you can't stop me!'

She stomped up the stairs, repeating as she went, 'You can't stop me! I'm having a shower, I am!'

Somehow Danielle had convinced herself she'd won the 'argument', but I knew I'd learned a valuable lesson that morning. Danielle liked to do the opposite of what you asked her to do, and I reckoned I'd have to keep that knowledge up my sleeve and use it wisely when I wanted to get her to behave the way she needed to.

It was mid-morning by the time we walked into town, leaving Jonathan in charge of the shop, but unfortunately it was far from the lovely stroll I'd envisaged. Danielle had a very annoying habit of walking too close to me and criss-crossing in front of me without warning. I was on alert the whole time, trying to avoid bashing into her or tripping over her. She also let her nose run and didn't seem to notice.

'Here's a tissue.'

'What's that for?'

'To blow your nose.'

'It doesn't need blowing. Honestly, you're such a fusspot, Angela.'

Eventually Danielle took the tissue I offered, made a

rather disgusting noise as she blew her nose and then tried to hand the wet tissue back to me.

'Please keep hold of that until we find a bin, Danielle.'

'Oh God, do I have to do everything around here?'

Almost as soon as we arrived on the high street two girls ran up to us.

'Hey, Danielle! Do you want to come round town with us?'

'Yeah!' she grinned. 'Come on!'

Danielle seemed to completely forget I was by her side, but one of her friends looked in my direction and laughed, saying to Danielle, 'Do you need to check first?'

I smiled and introduced myself as Angela. I never say I'm a foster carer as I feel it's up to the child to decide what they tell their friends, and when. I've learned that most children prefer not to flag up the fact they are in foster care, especially at the beginning of a new placement, and very rarely when they are in a temporary placement.

Danielle explained that she knew the girls – Shelby and Mina – from a previous school, and the girls were quick to point out that it was a teacher-training day and they were not playing truant.

'We're just going to get a drink in the cafe and go round the market, if you can come with us?' Mina said.

'Is that OK?' Danielle asked.

'Actually,' I said, thinking on my feet, 'I wanted to buy you a few things and we haven't got long. Can you fix something up for another day?'

Danielle looked very unhappy with this but then Shelby deffused the situation by reminding the group that the youth club was on that night.

'Never mind,' she said. 'Are you coming tonight? We can all catch up then. It'll be a laugh.'

'Is THAT OK?' Danielle asked me pointedly.

'I'm sure it's fine,' I said.

As the placement was so new and I had so little information about Danielle I didn't want to let her out of my sight in town, but the social workers had said nothing about restricting her from any supervised activities, despite her exclusion from school. Danielle and her friends had clearly been to the youth club together before, and I knew it well. There were always a few people I'd known for years taking the money on the door, signing the kids in and keeping an eye on things. I also knew it was a secure environment as I'd worked there myself as a volunteer on many occasions in the past. Nevertheless, I made a mental note to put a quick call in to our support social worker, Nelson, just to be sure Danielle was allowed to attend.

'So I can go?'

'I'm sure it's fine,' I repeated, telling her we'd work out the arrangements later. Danielle seemed satisfied with this.

'See you there,' the girls said. 'Be there or be square!'

All three girls giggled, and as soon as they were out of sight Danielle looked at me very seriously and said, 'So what's all this stuff you're buying for me, Angela?'

She wasn't daft, this girl!

'Well, I thought we'd get some stationery, as I expect you'll be needing that.'

'Why?'

'Because you're not at school at the moment.'

'So?'

'Well, I imagine you'll be sent some work to do at home, to keep you going while the school situation is sorted out. That's what normally happens if a child can't go to school.'

'Are you joking?'

'No, I'm not. I'm not sure how it will work out, but I do know Social Services won't want you to miss out on your education. So, come on, let's get you some essentials, shall we?'

I steered Danielle into WHSmith and her eyes lit up.

'Can I have one of these?'

She was looking at a notepad that came with a stamper set, so you could customise it with your name.

'Yes,' I said. 'And how about these pens?'

A huge smile spread across Danielle's face. I'd selected a pack of brightly coloured pens with silly animal heads stuck on their tops.

'Wicked!' she said. 'You're not as boring as I thought you were, Angela.'

'Thanks!' I grinned. 'Best compliment I've had all day!'

When we got home Danielle immediately set about stamping her name on her new book. She appeared to have forgotten all about her hamster and made no mention of him or the untouched carrots on the floor. Instead, she sat herself at the kitchen table, engrossed in choosing which style of lettering she was going to use for her name.

I slipped out to call Nelson and ask about the youth club, and was kept on hold for about fifteen minutes before being told there was no problem at all with Danielle meeting her friends there. Nelson was in a rush and I arranged to call him on Monday to have a further discussion, when he would be in the office all morning and would have more time. As I stepped back into the kitchen, Danielle looked very proud as she held her notepad up for me to see.

'Finished!' she declared cheerfully.

I was surprised to see that the surname Danielle had printed wasn't the one I'd seen on her paperwork from Social Services, and so I asked her casually if she used two different names, which often happens when children come from broken homes.

'Yes,' she said. 'But this is the surname I'm going to use from now on, because it's the name of my forever family.'

4

'I'm not staying here'

'Angela, come quick! I've found Scooter!'

Danielle had gone upstairs to get ready for the youth club, and she called me into her room. When I opened the door I saw her standing by the bed, holding the hamster to her chest.

'Wow! That's great news, and how lucky he didn't go far. He must like it in your room. Most hamsters would be off like a shot, given half the chance.'

'I know. Very lucky, wasn't it?'

She gave me one of those slightly suspect-looking smiles again, and something told me Danielle wasn't giving me the full story. I flicked my eyes around the room and noticed that her underwear was in a pile on the floor, beside the chest of drawers. One of the drawers was open just enough for me to see a handful of straw and a sprinkling of hamster food inside.

'Gosh!' I exclaimed, stepping towards the open drawer.

'Look at this, Danielle. Anyone would think he'd tried to make this drawer his new home.'

She blushed and looked to the floor. 'Oh, you could be right. Er, I'm glad my stuff wasn't in there. He was clever to do that, wasn't he?'

'Well, maybe he was,' I said.

It appeared very obvious that Danielle had hidden Scooter in the drawer herself, but I didn't know that for certain and so I had to tread carefully. I knew from my experience and training that accusing a child of telling fibs or even doubting their word could do a lot of damage, so I would never go down that road unless I was one hundred per cent sure of the facts. I needed Danielle to feel comfortable with me, and to trust me, in case she wanted to disclose anything or had any questions to ask me.

'Now, let's clear all this mess up. And if I were you I wouldn't leave your drawers empty or open again. I think if you keep your things in their place, there's a better chance Scooter will stay in his place, don't you?'

'I suppose.'

As I began picking up the underwear to put it back in Danielle's drawer I noticed that some of her knickers were damp and smelt of urine.

'Oh dear,' I said. 'I thought this was all clean underwear.'

'It is,' Danielle replied defiantly.

'I don't think so. It's damp and it doesn't smell fresh.'

'It's fine. The smell is Scooter! He must have weed! Just put it in the drawer, will you?'

'No, Danielle. We need to sort this out. I wouldn't like you to put on underwear that isn't clean and dry.'

'Oh *wouldn't* you, Saint Angela!'

'Please don't be rude to me, Danielle. I'm trying to help you, because I care about you and I want the best for you.'

'I've already told you; I just want to go back to my forever family. I know your game, Angela.'

Danielle put her hands on her hips and looked at me accusingly. She also stepped up very close to me, so her face was inches from mine.

'Game?' I repeated back, with a question in my voice.

'Yes. YOUR GAME! I spoke to them last night. They told me everything.'

'They told you everything?'

Danielle now spoke to Scooter, holding him in front of her face.

'You heard me, didn't you, Scooter? You heard what I heard?'

She then put on a strange, faraway voice.

'I'm your forever mum, Danielle. Angela and Jonathan are only looking after you for the money. Mike and me don't get paid. We looked after you for free, not like them!'

I knew full well that all foster carers receive payment, regardless of the length of a child's stay or the type of care order the child is under. Just because Danielle's previous carers had planned to be her forever family made no difference; they would still have received payment. I had no idea if Danielle was telling the truth about this conversation, but nevertheless I wanted to make it clear where we stood.

'Danielle, Jonathan and I are looking after you because we want to help you. We don't do this job for the money. We have a successful business in our flower shop. We love fostering and we want to care for you. That is why we are foster carers. We want to help you. That is our priority, and that is the truth of the matter.'

Danielle thought about this for a moment or two before looking me in the eye, very seriously.

'Honest?' she asked, using her own voice again.

'Honestly, yes.'

'In that case I'll have to phone Glennis back and ask her what she was on about, because she definitely said her and Mike don't get paid and you do it for the money!'

'Phone them back?' I questioned.

'Yes. I wasn't lying about speaking to them, you know. I didn't make it up! I phoned them last night, on my mobile.'

'Right. OK. Thanks for telling me that.'

'Is there a problem?'

'Just leave it with me.'

I didn't know what to think and I didn't understand why Danielle was clinging on to her forever family when the placement had broken down and she had left their home. In fact, I was struggling to get a handle on Danielle for lots of reasons. One minute she was seemingly being very open and childlike with me, the next I didn't have a clue if she was telling lies, or what games she might be playing. Now it seemed she was acting more like a manipulative teenager than a vulnerable young girl, and I was growing increasingly confused by her behaviour.

What was very clear, even in the absence of any further information from Social Services, was that Danielle had a lot of issues. I imagined she must have suffered some kind of trauma in her life, perhaps a very serious one. Just going into care at the age of five was traumatic enough, whatever the reason behind it. What's more, Danielle's basic manners were poor for a twelve-year-old, and her personal hygiene left a lot to be desired. Communicating with her was like walking a tightrope: you just never knew whether you'd manage to hold on until the end of a conversation, or whether she'd plummet into a world of confusing nonsense at any minute, trying to pull you in with her.

The rude way Danielle had spoken to me at various points in the day could easily have provided good reason for me to stop her going to the youth club, but I felt this was not the way to play things with her. My instincts told me that any consequences we were going to introduce to try to improve this young lady's behaviour would have to be very well thought out, and Jonathan agreed. We could see we'd have a battle on our hands if we didn't deal with things in the right way, and we both felt we had to find out more about what had happened to Danielle in the past before we could put the best strategy in place to help her move forward.

Jonathan and I went together to drop Danielle off at youth club at 7 p.m. We both felt quite frazzled by that point in the day. Danielle had made dinner time rather unpleasant, saying the Parmesan cheese smelt like sick and pretending to throw up and making vomiting noises when she was eating her spaghetti Bolognese.

'Danielle, I have to remind you to keep your mouth closed when you're eating. It's not nice to see the contents of your mouth, or to hear you talk that way while we are eating.'

'Well why are you looking at me? I didn't ask you to look at me, or listen to me!'

She looked at me in the way a teacher might look at a petulant child, raising her eyebrows as if to say: 'Well? What's the explanation?'

I ignored this and told Danielle we'd been thinking about taking her out to a carvery we liked, where you could refill your plate as many times as you wanted.

'I'd like that,' she said. 'What's a carvery?'

I explained how you could choose the type of roast meat you wanted and help yourself to unlimited potatoes, vegetables, Yorkshire pudding and gravy.

'Can you cut your own meat and have more?'

'No, that's the only thing you can't help yourself to.'

'Well why did you say you can refill your plate as many times as you wanted if you can't have more meat?'

'Look, it would be good to take you there, Danielle. I think you'd really enjoy it. The food is delicious, but first I need to be sure you can display good table manners.'

'I can,' she said. 'But sometimes I just don't want to!'

'Thank God she's going out for a couple of hours!' Jonathan whispered to me later, as we cleared up the plates. 'I don't think my nerves can take much more!'

When we pulled up at the youth club we saw Mina and Shelby waiting outside, which is what the girls had arranged between themselves.

'OK, Danielle, we'll be back at 9 p.m. to collect you,' I said as we got out of the car to see her off. 'We'll be right here.'

We'd parked right in front of the building where the youth club was held and I made it clear we'd be in the same spot later. As Danielle had a mobile phone I also made sure I had her number and she had ours, as well as the home phone number. Then I handed Danielle £2.50, which was enough for her entrance fee and to buy a drink and a snack. She said thank you very politely, and Jonathan and I watched as the three girls went inside the hall, chatting happily and linking arms. Danielle was wearing clean clothes and I hoped to goodness she stayed dry while she was out.

'Fingers crossed she has a good time,' Jonathan said. 'With a bit of luck this will do her the world of good. It must be so unsettling for her, suddenly being with us, and being out of school.'

'I agree. It's impossible to put yourself in her shoes. Being in foster care is tough enough, as we've said so many times. But when a child thinks they have found a new home for life and everything is set up . . .'

Jonathan finished my sentence. 'And then that goes wrong. Well, it's no wonder she has issues.'

The two of us returned to the youth club together to collect Danielle at 9 p.m. but after waiting outside until the last children emerged, it suddenly dawned on us she wasn't coming out.

I went inside the hall, where a lady I'd known for many years was folding away the table that is always put up in the entrance. Two people generally sit there, signing the kids in and out and taking the money on the door.

'Jan,' I said, 'I've come to collect a young girl and she's not here. Did you see her?'

I described Danielle and her two friends and gave their arrival time so Jan could check her register.

'Sorry, Angela, they didn't sign in,' she said, scouring the list of names in her book. 'We didn't have many in tonight so even if they came in without signing in, I'd have noticed them. So sorry, Angela, the three girls weren't here.'

My heart fell to my feet. *What an idiot! Why didn't I make sure I saw them sign in?*

I looked at Jonathan, who was already on his mobile, calling Danielle. It went straight to voicemail.

'Where is she?' I said.

We had experience of kids going missing for days, not coming home until the early hours and even of taking calls from hospitals and the police, telling us to come and collect a child in our care who had been taken to A & E or been arrested. It was par for the course, unfortunately, but I hadn't seen this coming. Danielle was twelve years old and had a naive side to her that worried me greatly. Her behaviour could be erratic and she was volatile too. We'd known her for such a short time and I had no idea what she was capable of.

'Look,' Jonathan said, calmly. 'Danielle knows her way to our house from town. Let's go home and see if she's decided to walk back with her friends.'

I agreed. It was still light and there was no point in raising the alarm and calling Social Services just yet, as Jonathan might well be right. With a bit of luck, we might even see the three girls in town together as we navigated the one-way system back to our house, as it took you on a convoluted route around our small town.

My eyes were on stalks the whole way home as Jonathan drove around the town. There was no sign of Danielle, and when we got back to the house I called her name as soon as I opened the front door.

'Danielle? Are you here? Can you hear me?'

Danielle didn't have her own key but I'd explained to her, as I do to all the children staying with us, that if they were ever locked out by accident they could always collect an emergency key from my mother, whose house was very close by.

We felt it was a sensible back-up plan, and my mum was happy to help. She had been passed by Social Services to be a babysitter for any children in our care and I had written down Mum's address and home phone number for Danielle on her first day with us, just in case she needed it.

I was aware I was clutching at straws but I hoped Danielle had fetched the key from Mum and I'd find her sitting in her bedroom, innocently playing with Scooter. Still calling her name, I ran to the top floor of our house and pushed open Danielle's bedroom door. The room was empty and exactly as she'd left it. There was no message on the answer-phone either, or on my mobile, and I knew that Mum would have tried to contact me if she'd given Danielle a key or had had a call or a knock on the door from her.

'She's not here!' I called down to Jonathan.

He didn't reply, and as I walked towards the last flight of stairs leading to the hallway I realised why. Jonathan had remembered Danielle had called one of her friends shortly before she went to the youth club, and while I was checking the bedroom he had phoned the last number dialled from our home phone.

'Thank you very much indeed!' Jonathan was saying, smiling at me and giving me the thumbs-up. 'That's very kind of you, Mrs Bashir. Oh, yes, I can see them pulling up. Thanks again. Much appreciated. Bye now.'

Jonathan looked at me with relief etched on his face.

'Mina's father is bringing her home. The girls decided to watch a film at Mina's instead of going to the youth club, because there were hardly any other kids there they knew, apparently, and they didn't fancy it.'

'Great,' I sighed, throwing open the front door to see Danielle stepping out of Mina's dad's white van.

Jonathan went out to say thank you to Mr Bashir while I waited at the door to greet Danielle.

'Hi, Angela!' she smiled breezily.

'Come on in,' I said, not looking best pleased.

'What's your problem?'

'Please don't speak to me in that rude way, Danielle. My "problem" is that I've been worried about you. We made an arrangement to collect you from the youth club but you didn't go, and didn't tell us what you were doing or how you were getting home. When we phoned your mobile it went straight to voicemail.'

'Oh!' she said, looking genuinely surprised. 'I didn't think of that. What time is it?'

'Quarter to ten. I was very worried when I discovered you didn't sign in at the youth club.'

'But why?' She was chewing her lip now and looking confused. 'I was with Mina and Shelby. Does it matter that I was in Mina's house instead of in the youth club? And it's not even THAT late. What's the big deal?'

'Yes it does matter, because Jonathan and I were worried when we got to the youth club and there was no sign of you, and you didn't answer your phone. If you look at it from our point of view, we haven't seen you since we dropped you off at 7 p.m., and that's nearly three hours ago. We need to know where you are, that you are safe and how you are getting home. It's very important, for your safety. Do you understand?'

Danielle nodded.

'Yes. Sorry. It won't happen again. My mobile was dead. I forgot to charge it before I went out.'

She gave me a sweet smile and apologised to Jonathan when he reappeared.

'Right, I'm tired,' she then announced. 'I'm going straight to bed.'

Jonathan and I both said goodnight politely as she headed up the stairs. I was just thinking to myself, *All's well that ends well*, when Danielle suddenly stopped dead, turned to face us and put her hands on her hips.

'Do you want to know why it won't happen again?' she shouted. 'Because I'm not staying here. I'm going back to my forever family. At least they know how to look after me properly. They wouldn't be so useless! It wouldn't take them nearly three hours to realise I was missing! And they don't even get paid!'

Danielle span around and stomped off as fast as she could to the top floor of the house, slamming her bedroom door after her. Jonathan put his arm around me. I didn't have to tell him how I felt, because I knew he was feeling equally bruised and deflated.

'This is not easy,' I said eventually, when we sat alone together in the kitchen, drinking tea and eating toasted teacakes. 'You certainly need a very thick skin to be a foster carer!'

I plastered my teacake with butter and Jonathan raised an eyebrow cheekily. We were both trying to keep hold of our sense of humour. It's often a saving grace when things get tough; although the reality was that we were both feeling the strain quite acutely that night.

'Comfort eating, Angela?' Jonathan teased.

'Yes, and don't look at me like that because I think I need it! Seriously, this is really not easy at all, is it?'

'No, it's not. It's a challenge, but do you know what?'

'Go on.'

'I really do hope Danielle can stay for a while, because I want to help her.'

'Yes. I totally agree with you, Jonathan. That's exactly how I feel.'

We sat in comfortable silence for a while, sharing the knowledge that come what may, helping children like Danielle was our role in life – a role we embraced, despite the difficulties we faced. We had never encountered a child quite like Danielle before, and we acknowledged this and agreed we needed as much help and advice from Social Services as we could get.

I called Nelson first thing on Monday morning, explaining all about the different issues we'd had to deal with, such as Danielle's rudeness and apparent duplicity, her poor manners and hygiene problems, and the fact she said she had contacted her forever family and wanted to use their surname. I also described the youth club drama, plus yet another difficulty we'd encountered over the weekend: Danielle wet the bed.

I must have spoken to Nelson for a full five minutes, as there was so much to get across to him, even though Danielle had only been with us for a matter of days.

'I think you need to introduce a star chart,' Nelson said straight away. 'Give Danielle five stars to begin with, but take a star away if she misbehaves. The deal is that if she keeps hold of all her stars for the day, she gets a small treat or she can bank it, and put it towards a bigger reward at the end of the week. In addition, if she not only holds on to her stars but also is particularly well behaved, she gets extra stars. You can give her twenty pence per star, up to £1 a day.'

Jonathan and I were more familiar with giving stars out for good behaviour rather than taking stars away for poor behaviour. My immediate reaction was to feel uncomfortable about penalising a child like this, but I trusted Nelson's professional advice and assumed he knew a good deal more about Danielle and her past history and personality than we did.

When a child is in emergency respite care, foster carers like us are often given very limited information about a child's background and the problems they have encountered historically. The child deserves the right to privacy, and Social Services generally operate on a 'need to know' basis. Therefore it's wise to follow advice from a social worker, especially in the very early stages of a placement.

Nelson went on to say he had some good news. He told me that arrangements had been put in place for Danielle to start having two hours of tuition, once a week, at an education centre in town. This was the best Social Services could offer for the time being, while efforts were being made to find Danielle a permanent school place.

'Thanks,' I said. 'Let's hope Danielle's behaviour will improve when she has other things to focus on.'

'I hope so,' Nelson replied. 'And good luck with the star chart. It can work really well. I hope it does for you, Angela.'

I thanked Nelson and felt reassured by our chat. I hadn't found out any more detail about Danielle's past history, or the previous foster carers, but Nelson's positivity and the fact he didn't seem unduly concerned by anything I'd told him put my mind at rest.

'Hopefully this star chart will get things on track,' I said to Jonathan optimistically. 'It's such early days for Danielle. Maybe she's just having a few teething problems. I'm sure things will improve soon, and we might even get the honeymoon period, you never know!'

This so-called honeymoon period generally happens at the start of a placement, when a child is on best behaviour, trying to settle in and wanting to create a good impression. Often, once a child has gone through this stage, things get trickier as they flex their muscles and begin to push the boundaries. However, as we know all too well, there are no hard and fast rules in fostering, and no two placements are the same. Danielle was certainly not in a honeymoon period, but I lived in hope.

Jonathan smiled. 'I love your optimism, Angela,' he replied. 'I think you were at the front of the queue when it was being dished out!'

5

'I'm very pleased with what you've achieved'

'If I'm still here, can I go bowling with my friends at the weekend? It's Mina's birthday.'

'That sounds like a nice treat, and I'd love for you to go bowling, Danielle. The answer is yes, as long as you behave well between now and then.'

'I'm always well behaved!' she said, smiling audaciously.

I'd introduced Danielle to the star chart but unfortunately it wasn't going very well. She had been rude to me the night before when I caught her drawing with a felt-tip pen on the upholstered seat of one of our dining chairs. I took a star away and she became very angry.

'I don't know what you're making a fuss about,' she had snarled. 'It's only a few scribbles. You're looking for an excuse to tell me off!'

Now she had come down to breakfast smelling of urine after getting dressed without taking a shower, even though I'd talked to her several times about personal hygiene and she was going to her first tuition session that day. When I asked her to go back upstairs and shower she accused me of making a drama out of nothing and told me to keep my nose out of her business.

'Danielle, I can't ignore this,' I said gently. 'I'm not making a fuss for the sake of it. I want you to smell fresh and you need to be dry and comfortable. I wouldn't want your friends, your tutor or anyone else to notice you not smelling good. You need to have a shower every morning, and if you have an accident in the day you need to have another wash and put on fresh clothes.'

'I don't care though, Angela. Nobody cares! It's none of your business.'

'It is my business and I do care about you, Danielle. There's a practical side to this too. I need to wash your clothes and your bedding if they get wet.'

'Why?'

'Because if they stay wet they will smell and rot and we'll have to throw them away.'

'Rot? The only rot around here is the rot you're talking!'

'Please don't speak to me like that, Danielle. I'm on your side. I want to help you and look after you as well as I possibly can.'

'Yeah, right. I've had enough of this!' she shouted. 'I hate it here and I hate you! All you care about is making money out of me.'

I thought carefully about how to react. According to the rules Nelson suggested we follow, Danielle would have to lose a star for giving me cheek. I didn't think it was a good idea to remind her of this now. After what had happened the night before I imagined that taking away another star would only fuel her anger, which would not help matters. I was worried about getting her to tuition in a fit state to learn, as well as in clean clothes.

'OK, Danielle,' I said dramatically, throwing my hands in the air. 'If that's what you want, have it your way. Just go to your first tuition session smelling like you do. And leave the wet bed. Hopefully it will have dried out a bit by bedtime.'

It was a tactic I'd used before, of course, but I wasn't sure Danielle was going to fall for it a second time. To my relief, she did.

'Fine. Even if YOU don't care about me, I'm having a shower. You can't stop me, Angela. And I'm going to tell Jonathan how mean you are when I see him. Oh yes. I'll tell him. You won't like that, will you? I bet he'll be on my side! I like him better than you because he's not so MEAN!'

She was stomping up the stairs now, looking straight ahead as she shouted loudly.

'Please bring me your dirty things and I'll put the washing machine on before we go to tuition,' I called after her.

'All she does is nag, nag, nag,' Danielle said. She was still looking ahead, and it was as if she was talking to an imaginary figure on the stairs.

I went into the kitchen, counted to ten and thought about the star chart. I was worried about it and my instincts were telling me it was not going to work. It was unusual to use a star chart so early on in a placement and after the incident with the felt-tip pens the night before it seemed to me that Danielle viewed the chart as a stick rather than a carrot. Still, I trusted Nelson's advice and decided we should persevere, at least for a little while longer. I'd pick my moment and talk to Danielle about it later.

I hoped Social Services could help when it came to Danielle's problems with wetting the bed and having accidents during the day, perhaps by giving me some historic-information they may have had about these issues. Danielle had intimated to me she'd had the habits for years: 'Why are you so worried? I can deal with it myself, thank you very much! Nobody has ever nagged me all the time like you do. Get over yourself, Angela!'

Clearly, I couldn't use the star chart to encourage her to stay dry: I knew full well there are often psychological reasons behind a child wetting the bed at night, and behind a child of Danielle's age wetting herself in the daytime. Nelson had not given me any advice in that regard, other than to reassure me he would speak to Danielle's social worker, Susan, as soon as possible, to see if there was anything useful on file that he could pass on.

During a quiet moment to myself I thought about how Danielle somehow seemed to deliberately set out to cause trouble, particularly when she wanted to provoke a reaction in me. Were the two things connected – her bed-wetting and making trouble for me? I kicked this thought around my head that morning. Perhaps Danielle was capable of not wetting the bed or wetting herself in the daytime, but *chose* to do so, as a way of lashing out or causing trouble. Or was I overthinking this?

'Penny for your thoughts,' Jonathan said, when he walked into the kitchen.

I told him what was on my mind, as I always do.

'Yes,' he nodded. 'I can see why you could think along those lines. Danielle is very hard to work out. I'm feeling confused myself and looking for answers. I guess it's good to talk it over, but at the end of the day we can only work with the facts, and unfortunately we don't have very many of those yet. We must try to boost her self-esteem. Maybe that will help.'

I smiled. This was typical Jonathan, summing up the situation sensibly and reminding me to be conscious of the difference between fact and opinion.

We knew by now that we would have a placement meeting coming up in the next few weeks, with Nelson and Susan. There's normally a brief placement meeting within five days of the child's arrival, which we'd had. We were very willing to agree for Danielle to stay with us for longer than the initial weekend of respite care we'd been asked to provide, though we had no idea at this stage how long she might stay. After the initial placement meeting, full placement meetings are typically held approximately every six weeks. Sometimes you don't see a social worker in between these meetings, but we'd been told the first full placement meeting would happen much sooner than usual. It seemed we were already getting more support and a higher level of contact with Social Services than normal, which we were grateful for.

As far as Jonathan and I were concerned, this meeting, which would be held at a Social Services office, couldn't come soon enough. I had so many questions about Danielle and I really wanted to do my best by her. Now she had her tuition in place I imagined she'd be staying with us for a few more weeks, at the very least, so I wanted all the help, advice and information I could get hold of.

Jonathan and I both drove Danielle to tuition later that day. She was finally dressed in clean clothes and had even washed her hair, which I was pleased to see. She was quiet in the car all the way to town, and when we arrived at the education centre she was very polite to her new tutor, Miss Powell, who was waiting in a corridor next to the main reception. I was thankful Danielle was behaving herself, especially as Miss Powell was very young and shy, and my first impression was that the tutor was someone who could be easily upset or manipulated by Danielle, if she were in a difficult mood.

'We'll be back in two hours,' I said to them both. 'I hope the session goes well.'

'Thank you, Mrs Hart. We'll be right here when you return. Please, take a seat Danielle.'

The tutor motioned for Danielle to sit at a very small table in the corridor, next to where we were standing.

'We're working here?' Danielle said, looking down her nose at the table.

'Yes – er, it's not ideal, but I'm sure we'll be fine,' Miss Powell said, slightly sheepishly.

Jonathan and I said goodbye and walked away, leaving them to it. When we got back to the car we found that Danielle had left twisted-up bits of tissue all over the back seat. That's what she must have been doing when she was quiet in the back of the car. I scooped them up and put them in a carrier bag, ready to throw in the bin. I guessed she might have wanted me to get cross about this and tell her off, but I wasn't going to go down that route. It was just a bit of paper, and it was easily cleared away.

When we got home Jonathan went straight into the shop to give our assistant, Barbara, a break, and I did some housework. Danielle had given me her dirty laundry as I'd asked her to, and it was now washed and ready to be pegged on the washing line. I went up to Danielle's room to check her mattress and, thankfully, it had escaped a soaking. I always have a plastic-lined protective sheet over all the mattresses used by children in the house, just in case, and it had worked well. I opened the window to air the room then looked around for the towels Danielle had used for her shower. I'd explained I wanted her to keep her towels on the rail over the radiator in her bedroom and not in the bathroom. This is a rule I have with all the children. Jonathan and I have our own bathroom next to our bedroom on the floor below, so we don't have to worry about our towels being mistaken for anybody else's, but with children sharing the bathroom on the top floor I like to be sure there are no mix-ups.

'Why do I need to bother?' Danielle had challenged when I explained the rule. 'I might as well leave my towels in the bathroom. There's only me using it.'

'No, please keep them in your room. Then if another child comes to stay you won't have to change what you're doing.' I explained that we had enough room in the house for another two children to stay if need be, adding, 'Usually, we do have more than one child staying with us.'

'I don't think they will ask you to have another child while I'm here,' Danielle had said flatly.

'You don't think so?'

'No. You don't know, do you, Angela?'

'I don't know what?' I said. I didn't want to ask any leading questions, because I sensed Danielle could be thinking about making some sort of a disclosure and I didn't want to put words in her mouth.

'What I mean is, you don't know why, Angela, do you? You don't know why Social Services won't ask you to have another child while I'm here.'

'I don't know why, Danielle.'

As we spoke I began to fold up some towels and load them into the ottoman we had on the landing, which was full of clean laundry. I busied myself deliberately, knowing that sometimes it's easier for a child to speak about a sensitive matter if they don't have to look at you and if you don't give them eye contact.

'Ask Susan!' Danielle had said, with a mischievous note in her voice.

'Ask Susan?'

'Yes. Ask Susan.'

Danielle ran to her dressing table, peered at her face in the mirror and began talking to herself as she examined her skin. It was greasy-looking, and she had a crop of spots on her forehead, beneath her fringe. 'Look at you, Danielle. Oooh, that's a nasty spot. Need to get rid of that. Now what was I doing . . .'

That was the end of the conversation. I had been left wondering if Danielle was maybe just seeking attention with the mysterious comments she made, or whether there was some truth in what she had suggested. My gut feeling was she was being a bit of a drama queen and trying to wind me up, but I wasn't sure.

Anyhow, after our chat Danielle did eventually agree to keep all her towels in her room, and that's why I was looking for them now. I'm very used to children leaving wet towels in a heap on the floor or on top of their duvet, and hanging them up is something I do almost on autopilot, because I've done it so many times.

Danielle had chosen to use a striped purple and white set, but none of the towels were anywhere to be seen. I went into the bathroom and had a quick scan around. I noticed the shower gel, shampoo and conditioner bottles were all empty in the bin, and I sighed because I knew they had been full up the night before.

We'd had several different children staying with us previously who couldn't resist playing with the toiletries in the bathroom, and by that I mean squirting them up the walls, pouring them down the plughole or, on one occasion, depositing whole plastic bottles down the toilet or even hiding them in the cistern. For this reason I only ever stock the children's bathroom with the minimum of essentials, in small-sized bottles. Razors, tweezers, nail scissors or anything remotely sharp are kept locked away in a cabinet in my room, as required by Social Services, and I have learned from experience not to leave too many toilet rolls, tissues or packs of cotton buds or cotton wool in the children's bathroom either, as in the past they have been wasted in various ways. For instance, once I found large wads of tissues blocking the sink. I've also discovered whole bags of cotton wool thrown down the toilet, cotton buds littering the shower tray or shoved up taps, and bits of sodden tissues slung at the walls and ceiling. I've even had to retrieve knickers out of the toilet in the past, and on one particularly memorable occasion, three toilet rolls from a brand-new pack were unfurled from the bathroom window. The pink tissue ended up caught in shrubs and trees and all over the lawn, and not just in our garden but in next-door's too. It was raining, and Jonathan and I had had quite a job on our hands clearing up. We ended up retrieving soggy lumps of tissue for days afterwards.

After failing to find Danielle's towels I went to fetch her a fresh set from the ottoman.

'Oh!' I exclaimed to myself when I opened the lid. Inside were Danielle's wet towels, and on top of them was a pair of urine-soaked pyjamas. She must have gone through two pairs the previous night, I realised, as I'd washed one pair that morning.

I wasn't sure what to make of this. I guessed it could be a deliberate attempt to irritate me, or perhaps Danielle knew no better and had got confused between the laundry bin and the ottoman?

When I first started fostering, my natural instinct was to go with the common-sense explanation. Back then, I'd have thought that no twelve-year-old child could accidentally make such an obvious mistake as that, but now I know better. Sadly, lots of children are never taught the basics of hygiene and need to learn everything from scratch. We've looked after children who have never been taught how to clean their teeth or had it explained to them why they need to wipe their bottoms and wash their hands after going to the toilet.

One boy drank some stagnant water from a bucket in the garden, as he couldn't be bothered going to the kitchen to get a drink. He said it was 'too much like hard work' and I remember asking, 'What, opening the door and going to the kitchen?' His response was, 'Yes, because I was too busy playing in the garden.'

He was genuinely surprised to hear how dangerous it could be to drink dirty water, because nobody had explained this to him before.

By the time I'd dealt with all the laundry it was time to collect Danielle from tuition. Miss Powell looked happy and relaxed as Jonathan and I walked down the corridor, and Danielle had her nose in a book and seemed to be concentrating hard. We hovered a few metres away in the corridor, not wanting to interrupt, and after a minute or two Danielle looked up and spotted us.

'Can I go now?' she asked Miss Powell.

'Yes, Danielle. And well done today. I'm very pleased with what you've achieved.'

Miss Powell handed Danielle a worksheet and signalled to Jonathan and me to come over.

'This is to be completed at home. Danielle's done really well. She has a super imagination!'

'Well done!' Jonathan and I said in unison.

I was really pleased about this. I wanted to be able to praise and reward Danielle, rather than take away stars and punish her.

We walked to the car, and Danielle seemed in a buoyant mood.

'I like Miss Powell,' she said. 'She said I'm good at writing stories.'

'That's great to hear. Is English one of your favourite subjects?'

'Yes. I love writing stories. She tells me what to write.'

'And what *has* Miss Powell asked you to write about for your homework?'

'I've got to fill a whole side of paper. I need to write about something I really like, and something I don't like. And I have to use lots of describing words.'

'Adjectives,' I said.

'Yes, them.'

Danielle got straight on with her homework as soon as we got home. For something she liked, she chose to write about her favourite television show, which was *EastEnders*. For something she didn't like, she wrote about cabbage and sprouts, although she told me she had never eaten either. Her language was basic and even babyish in places and her handwriting looked like the work of a much younger girl, but in my book she scored ten out of ten because she put a lot of effort into her work. The only thing Danielle hadn't done was to underline all the adjectives, as she'd been asked to do. When I pointed this out, suggesting this would be the finishing touch and would please Miss Powell, she refused point-blank to do it, even when I offered her the use of my brand-new pink highlighter pen.

'No, I've done enough,' she said flatly.

'But it'll be *perfect* if you do that, and it won't take long at all. Why not finish it off properly?'

'No. I've done enough,' Danielle reiterated. 'I don't want to do any more.'

I had another go at trying to persuade her a bit later on with no luck, and I wondered why she seemed to be deliberately derailing her chances of handing in an excellent piece of work. However, when I reflected on this later I kicked myself, because I realised I should not have pushed Danielle to produce perfect work. She'd done far more than I'd expected, and why had I projected my own standards on to her? It was a mistake, and a lesson learned for me. Danielle had done well and I should have focused on what she'd achieved, not what was lacking.

I picked my moment to talk to Danielle about the laundry and the importance of keeping wet things away from the clean, dry linen and towels. I brought it up when she was having a cup of tea and a snack, looking relaxed at the kitchen table, but Danielle pretended she didn't hear me.

'Danielle, did you hear what I said about the laundry?'

She stared into space, a frozen expression on her face.

I needed to go to the toilet, so I nipped to the bathroom upstairs, deciding I'd count to ten and try again when I returned. As soon as I locked the bathroom door I heard Danielle outside.

'Angela, Angela, what did you say?'

'Just a minute, I'll be down in a minute!'

'I want to know what you were saying! What did you say?'

'Hold on!'

'Is it about the laundry?'

'Yes! Give me a moment. I'm just washing my hands.'

'Can I come in?'

'No. Wait there,' I said, thinking it was a good job I always locked the door. 'I'm finished now.'

When I opened the bathroom door Danielle was standing right in front of me, blocking my way.

'Shall we go back to the kitchen?' I said, gesturing at her to move away and head down the stairs.

I'd chosen to use my bathroom on the first floor as I'd got used to Danielle following me whenever I needed to go to the toilet; she did it every day. I thought I stood a better chance of having some privacy if I avoided the downstairs loo.

'OK,' she said, moving aside just enough to let me step out of the bathroom. I led the way downstairs and Danielle followed, so close behind I thought she was going to tread on my heels. Then she pushed past and overtook me, stopping dead on the stair in front of me, which took me by surprise and forced me to stop in my tracks.

'Let's not have any accidents on the stairs,' I said, grabbing the banisters.

Danielle turned to face me, hands on hips, and said, 'You were getting in my way, Angela!'

'Danielle, please turn round. It's not safe to stand backwards on the stairs.'

She huffed and did as I asked. Once again I counted to ten in my head – or perhaps it was twenty that time! – and when we were back in the kitchen I returned to the conversation about the laundry, trying to get across to Danielle how important it was to keep clean linen away from dirty laundry.

'OK,' she said, raising her eyes to the ceiling. 'I wasn't sure what that otter thing was for. What did you say it was?'

'The ottoman? Oh yes. It's useful. I always keep it stocked up, so you always know where to find clean sheets and so on.'

'You're *so* organised,' Danielle said sweetly, giving me a broad smile. 'If only we were all like you!'

'I've had years of practice,' I replied. It was difficult to work out if Danielle was paying me a compliment or taking the mickey.

'More tea?' I asked, giving her an equally broad smile and helping myself to another biscuit.

I had told the social workers I wanted to make an appointment for Danielle with the doctor, so she could get some help with her wetting problem. I brought this up with Danielle the day after we discussed the laundry, and thankfully she was in a fairly good mood. She'd had a shower and washed her hair, and she was sitting at the kitchen table, eating some crumpets she'd smeared with an extremely thick layer of peanut butter.

'How are you feeling this morning?' I asked.

'I'm not sure. How do you know?'

'Well, do you feel good? Did you sleep OK?'

Not for the first time I'd heard her pacing around late into the night, but when I finally went upstairs to investigate I saw her light hastily go off.

'Yes, I slept fine. I feel OK, thanks. I didn't have a nightmare.'

'You didn't have a nightmare?'

'No. I'm good.'

I made a mental note to try to find out more about these possible nightmares and what caused her to be restless at night. She clearly didn't want to elaborate now, and so I moved the conversation on.

I explained to Danielle that I was hoping we could improve things for her, in terms of her bed-wetting and incontinence, by going to see the doctor. She didn't argue, but she didn't exactly look pleased at the idea, and who could blame her? It was unusual for a child of twelve to have such a problem, day and night, and of course having to talk about this with a doctor could not have been an appealing prospect for her. I tried my best to focus on how it was all for her benefit, and how much better she would feel when the problem was under control – which I was sure it could be – but she didn't look convinced.

After that we had a pleasant couple of days with Danielle, with very few arguments and largely good behaviour. She happily played dominoes with my mum for hours one afternoon, although I think it worked well largely on account of Mum being incredibly patient.

'It's your turn, dear!' Mum said to chivvy Danielle gently along whenever she took rather too long to go.

'I'm thinking!' Danielle said.

I was doing some paperwork at the other end of the dining table as they played, and I had a very good idea what was going on here: the more Mum encouraged Danielle to hurry up, the longer she took to place her next domino. I guessed Danielle wanted to be in control of the game, and thanks to Mum's good nature she was. Mum wasn't worried how long the game took or who was 'in charge', and perhaps that was why Danielle got on so well with my mother.

Looking at them play, I wished I could get along with Danielle as well as my mum did, but as Jonathan pointed out: 'Letting Danielle be in control of a game of dominoes is one thing. It's an entirely different matter when it comes to eating, doing homework, keeping clean and all those other essential things we have to help her with.'

He was right. I couldn't let Danielle be in charge in her day-to-day life. It was obvious that in her past she'd missed out on being taught some of the basic rules of society – or that perhaps she'd been led to believe that some of the rules she lived by were normal and acceptable, when they were anything but.

At the weekend, thanks to her good behaviour, I was happy to drop Danielle at Mina's house for the birthday bowling party she had been invited to. She'd spent some of her pocket money buying Mina a card, and I'd given her some extra money to pay for a small gift.

'Perhaps we've turned a corner,' I said to Jonathan, sighing with relief when Danielle returned from the party. She was full of stories about who scored a strike and what they'd had to eat and drink, and it was great to see her having such a good day.

'I hope you're right,' Jonathan said. 'Maybe all she needed was to be given more praise and encouragement. Perhaps Miss Powell has boosted her self-esteem by remarking on her good work at tuition? Let's hope the worst is behind us. It certainly looks promising.'

I really hoped Jonathan could be right. I felt that when Danielle arrived she'd expected not to like us, and it was my guess she imagined she'd be told off and punished for every shortcoming – even the ones she had no control over. She was starting to see that wasn't the case and that in fact Jonathan and I don't even use the word 'punishment', preferring to talk about consequences, or better still to focus on the positive benefits and rewards that follow good behaviour.

That night Danielle told us she wanted to carry on living with us after all.

'My friend said I'm lucky to be here,' she said. 'I don't think I'm lucky. But I want to stay.'

I wasn't quite sure what to make of that, but this reinforced our hopes we'd turned a corner with Danielle. I felt quietly optimistic.

6

'How can I be good?'

After Danielle had been with us for just under three weeks we were asked to attend our first full placement meeting with her social worker, Susan, our support social worker, Nelson, a family-aid worker called Deirdre, plus Miss Powell the tuition teacher. This came sooner than we expected – as I've said, they normally happen after six weeks – but Jonathan and I were certainly not complaining. Social Services had been very proactive, and even though we still had unanswered questions, we were grateful for all the contact we'd already had with Susan and Nelson in the short time Danielle had been with us.

In hindsight it's clear Social Services knew what a difficult child Danielle could be to look after, and I don't blame anyone for not telling us the full extent of how challenging she could be, right from the start. If social workers divulged every alarming detail about the potential problems a new foster child might bring they would have an almost impossible job on their hands in trying to place children with willing carers who had not been put off, or even frightened away.

In any case, over the years Jonathan and I have learned to make up our own minds with regard to what is already on file about a child. We've found it's not always helpful to read everything written. For example, notes from a previous carer, recorded after a placement breakdown, might focus on problems and negative issues, for understandable reasons. Living with the child is actually the best way of finding out what they are really like, and how they are in the present moment.

Susan had paid a visit to our home shortly before the placement meeting, and she sat Jonathan and me down and told us that Danielle had been abused. Sadly, this did not come as a surprise: in fact, it confirmed our growing suspicions. It was clear Danielle had suffered trauma in her life and unfortunately we've looked after enough abused children to know when a child has been damaged by physical, sexual or emotional abuse.

From her difficult and sometimes obstructive, rude and erratic behaviour and attitude, it was obvious that Danielle had been emotionally neglected at the very least, and when Jonathan and I went to one of our regular training sessions one afternoon, while Danielle went to the cinema with my mum to watch a rerun of *Grease*, a penny dropped.

The session was about attachment disorder, and hearing more about this condition made me realise Danielle showed a lot of signs that she suffered with attachment issues. We'd attended training sessions on attachment disorder previously, although I'm going back more than a decade when information was far more limited than it is today. Through our previous training, Jonathan and I already knew that attachment disorder happens when a child's basic needs are not met at a very early age, typically between birth and the age of five. The child may be left to cry with hunger, pain, discomfort or simply when they want a cuddle. When no adult pays attention and meets their needs, they learn to accept that they are not the priority to the adult or adults and, in severe cases – perhaps when physical or sexual abuse is also taking place – that the adults are a threat to them and cannot be trusted. This affects brain development and causes the child to instinctively deal with everyday life primarily in a way they think will keep them safe.

At this latest training session, Jonathan and I picked up more information, which was new to us at the time. We learned that children with attachment disorder – and particularly a severe form of it, called reactive attachment disorder – develop a deep-rooted habit of manipulating others in order to control their world in a way that will keep them safe from harm – or alive, even. The trainer explained that it is impossible for children suffering from reactive attachment disorder to form the kind of relationships the rest of us take for granted. They are out in the emotional wilderness, effectively, and without normal attachments their ability to trust others, accept boundaries or discipline, develop self-control or take on responsibility for their own actions is hugely impaired. The damage is not completely irreparable, but it takes a lot of work and professional intervention to turn a child around who has suffered such a devastating start in life.

When Susan told us Danielle had been abused my heart sank; having this confirmed was very upsetting, despite our suspicions. I took a breath, composed myself and asked Susan if Danielle had been diagnosed with attachment disorder, or reactive attachment disorder. I don't know why that was the first thing I asked, as I had a million questions running round my mind. In hindsight, perhaps I was stalling for time, as subconsciously I was putting off hearing the details of Danielle's abuse.

'No,' Susan said. 'But as you've seen, she shows some classic signs – the manipulative behaviour, for example.'

Susan explained that when Danielle was living with her supposed forever family, they raised similar concerns. Danielle had been seeing a therapist, but when her previous carers questioned whether she had attachment disorder, Danielle was examined by a specialist doctor and put under the care of a child psychologist, who was still in the process of assessing and diagnosing Danielle.

'The psychologist has been abroad on a course so she has missed a session, but ordinarily Danielle attends a session once a month. I will give you further details at the placement meeting,' Susan told us.

Despite recognising Danielle had been traumatised and recognising she'd suffered some kind of abuse in her early childhood, until this conversation with Susan, Jonathan and I could only guess at the specific type of abuse she had been subjected to. I had mixed emotions when Susan began to give us more details. I desperately wanted to know what had happened to Danielle in her past, so I could understand her and help her in the best possible way, but at the same time I wished I didn't have to hear this.

It's always difficult to bear, learning what a child has been subjected to, and it has never got any easier over the years. It's something I really did not bargain for when I first began to foster. I naively imagined the vast majority of children who needed foster care had lost their parents. I thought being an orphan or perhaps being the child of an unmarried mother who was struggling was the only reason a youngster would be placed in care or put up for adoption. Of course, that was not always the case even back then, and over the years changes in society have meant that nowadays it is very, very rarely the case.

Most children in care in this day and age do have parents and, needless to say, mothers do not give up their children simply because they are unmarried. Sadly, this means the majority of children who find themselves in the care system come from families that are dysfunctional in some way, and it follows that many of those children have suffered trauma in their lives and have behavioural or emotional problems as a result.

'Danielle was sexually abused,' Susan said solemnly. 'She had a dreadful start in life.'

I can still picture Susan clearly, shaking her head and looking very serious as Jonathan and I listened intently.

'How terribly sad,' I said. I was sitting on the sofa in our living room and I looked out of the window, out across the park and fields at the back of our house. There were young children playing on the slide and swings and kicking footballs. Innocent, happy little kids, who looked like they didn't have a care in the world. I thought about the fact Danielle had only been five years old when she was initially taken into care. Clearly she had been abused – sexually abused – at a very young age. What an absolute tragedy. I saw Jonathan swallow hard and clench his jaw. I'd seen him do that many times before: he was suppressing tears.

Susan and Nelson had both been very efficient in fixing up the upcoming placement meeting, and they made sure Jonathan and I could both attend, offering to provide a respite carer if need be, which I said was not necessary, as my mum was very happy to look after Danielle while we were out. Mum and Danielle got on so well, and every time I'd left them alone together Mum had said, 'She's been as good as gold!' They seemed to have a surprising number of things in common. For instance, they liked a lot of the same films and TV shows and, to Danielle's amazement, my mum was as big a fan of Robbie Williams as she was. They both liked Stevie Wonder and Dionne Warwick too. 'You couldn't make it up!' Jonathan had commented when he heard them talking about their favourite Motown album one day.

On the day of the placement meeting we left Mum and Danielle together at home, happily playing Scrabble. Danielle had never played the game before, and once again

Mum's patience was coming into its own as she explained the rules.

'But what's the point in having letters and not words?'

'Goodness, that's the whole point, Danielle! Here, let me have a look at your tiles. We'll play a practice round and see what we can come up with together.'

'Why are you being so nice to me?'

Mum seemed very amused by the question and she laughed. She had no idea what Danielle's life had been like or that she had trust and attachment issues, or any other issues for that matter. Refreshingly, Mum simply took the question at face value.

'What a funny question! Why would I not be nice? I want to have a good game of Scrabble with you. Now come on, let's get started!' I smiled. My mum had a wonderful way with Danielle.

The placement meeting was held in an old-fashioned, wood-panelled room within what was once the old town hall. My low heels clip-clopped on the hard oak floor as I crossed the echoey room with Jonathan at my side, and I made a note to myself as heads turned: *Wear your soft wedges next time you have to come in one of these big, old rooms, Angela!*

Seated around a large oval table in the centre of the room were Susan, Nelson, Miss Powell and a lady I'd never met before. Susan introduced us: this was Deirdre, the family-aid worker who was going to support us with some practical help. I immediately liked the look of Deirdre. She was the sort of person who smiled with her eyes, so you knew she was genuinely pleased to meet you.

Once the introductions were over Susan asked Jonathan and me to sum up how we felt things were going with Danielle.

'Things are going well at the minute, but generally speaking I'd say it's up and down,' I said, glancing at Jonathan as he tipped his head forward in agreement. 'I feel like whenever we make progress, something unexpected or disappointing happens and we're back to square one. We're on an up now. I feel things have improved and I'm optimistic we'll ultimately make more progress, but I'm not sure how steady that progress will be.'

Jonathan nodded. 'Some days it feels like climbing a mountain and sliding back down just before you get to the top.'

We both admitted we felt deflated when that happened and, prompted by Nelson, I gave an example.

'This is a typical scenario, which hopefully will make you see what Danielle is like. I've been encouraging her to help me cook and to eat healthy foods. Yesterday she threw herself enthusiastically into making a vegetable curry with me. We all sat down to eat together, but Danielle suddenly said she didn't like the curry and wasn't going to eat it. She insisted she wasn't hungry, although earlier on she'd told me she was starving and couldn't wait for the rice to be ready. After making a fuss for a while she said her meal had gone cold and asked if she could throw it in the bin and have something else later. She then said she didn't like the taste at all, even though when we were cooking, earlier on, she said it was delicious.'

I wondered if some of the people in the meeting were thinking, *Maybe she really didn't like it?* so I went on, to make sure I'd got my point across. 'What I'm saying is, it's difficult to know where you are with Danielle and whether she is telling the truth. I found her breakfast in the bin one day, though she told me she was full up after eating it. I don't know if she is trying to be difficult on purpose.'

Jonathan explained that one morning Danielle came downstairs and asked us, 'Who will I be today? The nice Danielle or the nasty Danielle?'

'I think that gives a good insight into what she is like,' he said.

'Yes,' I added. 'It's almost as if she doesn't want things to work. She looks for ways to create trouble, seemingly unnecessarily. I don't know if she does this in a deliberate, trouble-making way or whether maybe it's more subtle than that.'

I didn't normally go into such detail at meetings like this. It's more typical for me to feel slightly rushed and to use an economy of words – a bit like when you go to see the GP and you know you have to get straight to the point or you'll make the surgery run late for the rest of the day. However, I didn't feel rushed or under pressure at all at this meeting. Everybody present was looking very thoughtful and paying close attention to each word I was saying.

'What do you mean, Angela, in saying maybe it's more subtle than that?' Susan asked.

'I mean maybe Danielle genuinely can't help herself. Something makes her cause trouble. Maybe it's subconscious, I don't know. As we've already touched on, I wonder if she has some form of attachment disorder.'

Susan nodded and scribbled in her notebook before clarifying to the rest of the group that this was something Danielle's psychologist was looking into.

We were told Social Services were having a lot of difficulty finding a suitable school that would take Danielle. In the meantime, as well as continuing with her tutor, Miss Powell, Deirdre, the family-aid worker, would help support us. It was explained to us that Deirdre would take Danielle out on educational trips, play sports with her and help keep her occupied while she was out of school.

'I'm looking forward to it,' Deirdre said.

She smiled warmly and the corners of her eyes creased effortlessly into two neat fans. *There's a lady who's used to smiling*, I thought. Deirdre looked to be in her early forties, and she had an aura of calm around her. I told her I was looking forward to it too, which I was. I had a good feeling about Deirdre and I imagined Danielle would as well.

Next, Susan gave us contact details of a lady called Hatty Bamford, who was the former headmistress of one of the special schools Danielle had attended when she was younger. We learned that Mrs Bamford now worked as a volunteer for CAMHS – Child and Adolescent Mental Health Services – which are NHS services for young people with emotional, behavioural or mental health difficulties. Mrs Bamford had kept in contact with Danielle after she left her primary school several years earlier and she knew both sets of foster carers Danielle had stayed with in the past. It was suggested we could contact her if we needed any further support, as Mrs Bamford was more than happy to volunteer her help with Danielle and wanted to stay in touch.

'For example,' Susan explained, 'on a day when Deirdre is not working with Danielle and there is no tuition, Mrs Bamford might be able to provide an hour or two of respite care, or even a whole day, if needed. She and Danielle have a very good relationship and Danielle likes to spend time with Mrs Bamford.'

'Thank you. Is there any more you can tell us about Danielle?' I asked. 'Anything at all?'

Again, this was slightly out of character for me. Normally, protocol dictates that foster carers wait to be given information by Social Services, on the understanding that any relevant details will be shared at the appropriate time. Jonathan flicked me a sideways glance and I could tell he was thinking I was perhaps being a little too forward. By my standards I was, but something felt different about this meeting. The longer it went on, the more I was getting the feeling that Danielle was a particularly special case, though nobody was telling us precisely why. Obviously, when a child has been sexually abused at a very young age, that child needs extremely careful handling. I understood that very well, but there was something else, something I couldn't quite put my finger on. It felt like I'd been thrown a few pieces of a puzzle and was trying to work the whole thing out, feeling certain that something was missing.

If Danielle is a child in greater need than most, surely Jonathan and I need as much information as possible?

Naturally, I kept the thoughts that were running though my head to myself. I was aware I was probably overthinking things, because I wanted the very best for Danielle and was looking for every possible way to make things better for her.

I reminded myself that, at the end of the day, I trusted the professional team of people around this table. They clearly wanted the best for Danielle, just as I did, and they were all highly experienced at their jobs. I had to be patient, listen to the rest of the meeting and trust that Danielle was getting the highest level of care, from all quarters.

'I'm pleased we have the support in place,' Susan said, shuffling her papers. 'And I'm delighted to say Deirdre will do two afternoon sessions a week.'

'Here are my contact details,' Deirdre said brightly, handing me a card. 'Give me a ring, Angela, and we'll go through our diaries and work out what suits.'

Miss Powell had only taught Danielle for two sessions of tuition so far and didn't say much, other than to agree with my observation that Danielle appeared to be 'up and down'.

'The first session was great and the next was not very good. Danielle had done her homework and was in a receptive mood when she arrived, but during most of the session she seemed distracted and kept putting on silly voices and turning round.'

I felt this was not surprising, as Danielle was working in

a corridor with people going about daily chores passing by her all the time. I don't think I would have been able to concentrate if it was me, and I asked if a room could be found instead. Miss Powell said there was nothing available for the time being, but reassured me she would let me know if the situation changed and a quieter space became available.

'Thank you,' I said. 'I'm sure that would help Danielle focus on her work.'

To our relief, Nelson agreed it was a good idea to abandon the star chart. Jonathan explained that we felt it poured petrol on the flames whenever Danielle behaved badly and had a star taken away.

'We feel Danielle needs support, not penalising in any way at all,' I said.

Everyone present supported our decision to seek medical help for the bed-wetting and daytime incontinence, which Nelson had already endorsed. Finally, we were told Danielle would resume her monthly visits to her psychologist. Susan gave me the details of where and when the sessions took place and told me a support worker would take Danielle to and from the sessions. I was given this support worker's name and number, and then Susan brought the meeting to a close.

'How d'you think that went?' Jonathan asked when we climbed in the car.

'Not sure what to make of it, to tell the truth,' I replied.

'Mmmm,' he said, furrowing his brow.

'I like the look of Deirdre, and Hatty Bamford sounds

great. I think there's a lot Social Services aren't telling us just yet though. I think Danielle has suffered more than we dare to imagine. What do you think, Jonathan?'

'Mmmm,' he said again. After a pause he added, 'I couldn't agree with you more. But I don't blame them. We're still none the wiser about how long she'll be with us, are we? It's just a case of taking things one step at a time, isn't it?'

'Yes, you're right. We'll just have to wait and see what happens next. At least we know the basic facts, and we have a lot of support in place. All we can do is our best.'

When we got home we decided to have a barbecue, as the sun was shining.

'I love barbecues,' Danielle said, eyes widening. 'I LOVE them!'

She helped Jonathan set everything up while I made some fresh burgers and defrosted some hamburger buns from the freezer. We hadn't planned the barbecue because the weather forecast hadn't been as good as it turned out, so I was making do with what we had in. I invited Mum to stay and join us – the Scrabble game had only just finished by the time we returned. She said she'd love to stay, as Danielle had been such good company, and she popped home to pick some fresh herbs from her garden and to collect a block of chocolate and some marshmallows she had in the cupboard.

The barbecue was a great success. Danielle thoroughly enjoyed herself, especially when it came to putting the marshmallows on skewers, toasting them and dipping them in the melted chocolate. 'These are the best things I've ever tasted,' she said, eating one after the other until I had to tell her I thought she'd had enough.

Later that evening, when everything was packed away and Danielle, Jonathan and I were relaxing and watching *EastEnders*, I thought it was a good time to explain to her what was going to happen, at least in the short term. She listened quietly as I told her how her time would be organised to include the activity sessions with Deirdre, her tuition with Miss Powell, her therapy with the psychologist, once a month, and hopefully some trips out with Mrs Bamford.

'Who's Mrs Bamford?'

'Hatty Bamford, your old head teacher?'

'Oh. I just call her Hatty. I thought she hated me.'

'You thought she hated you?'

'Yes. She kicked me out of her school, didn't she!'

This was something I was not aware of and I wondered whether it was true or if she'd got things muddled up, having recently been excluded from her last school.

I told Danielle I understood she had kept in touch with Hatty and they had regular trips out together.

'We do. *I* like *her*. But she must hate me, mustn't she?'

I could feel myself getting pulled into a muddled nonsense conversation and I wondered if Danielle was deliberately trying to confuse me or wind me up.

Here we go again, I thought. *One step forward, two steps back. What a shame after such a lovely barbecue!*

Danielle had proved to be very adept at lapsing into nonsense conversations and trying to drag others in with her, but they were never helpful and so I made sure I trod carefully, sticking to the facts and trying to steer the conversation back on track.

'Social Services have given me Hatty's phone number and I was going to ring her and see if we can fix up an outing for the two of you. She wants to see you. That's what your social worker said. Hatty is looking forward to seeing you and she very much enjoys spending time with you.'

'Great! I'd like that. Thank you.'

That was how chats with Danielle often went. One minute she was overcomplicating things or talking almost in rhymes, or at least that's how it seemed. Then the next it was as if she'd had a sudden flash of clarity, good manners or both. It meant that, just as she sometimes asked herself *Who will I be?*, I found myself wondering which Danielle would reply to me. On many occasions I had a slightly nervous feeling in my stomach, hoping Danielle would be pleasant and not snap or be rude, never quite knowing which way our conversation would go.

There was a music festival in the town, and I told Danielle she could go with Mina and Shelby, provided her behaviour was good over the next few days.

'How can I be good?' she asked, looking genuinely confused.

'By doing as you're asked,' I said breezily. 'It's really not that difficult. You behaved beautifully at the barbecue and when you were playing Scrabble with my mum. I know you can behave, and you were very helpful too.'

'OK. So what do I have to do now? Are you setting me a trap?'

'A trap? No, not at all. Why would I do that? I want you to behave well and I want to be able to let you go to the festival. There's nothing I'd like more.'

'So what's the catch?'

'No catch. I know you have to finish the homework Miss Powell set at your last tuition session, and I would like you to do your very best to keep yourself clean, have showers every morning and let me know when I need to wash your bedding.'

'That's easy!'

'Good, I'm glad you think so. And it goes without saying that I'd like good manners at all times – and especially at the table.'

'I can do that!'

'I know you can.'

'So I don't have to do any extras?'

'Extras?'

'Yes, you know. Will you give me money for extras?'

'Oh, I see. You mean chores? I tell you what, Danielle, provided you do all I've asked you to do, I will give you some extra pocket money if you do a few small things to help me and Jonathan around the house.'

She rolled her eyes.

'Here we go. Slave labour! They told me you'd do this.'

'They told you?'

'Glennis and Mike. They said you would use me like a skivvy! They said it happens all the time. People like you con their way into becoming foster carers just so they can lock kids in the house and get them to scrub the floor and do all the shit jobs!'

'Danielle! Please do not use language like that. I'm upset that you're saying such things. I've told you before. Jonathan and I enjoy being foster carers. We do it for love, not money. If you don't want me to give you a couple of little jobs to do, so you can earn extra money for the music festival, that's fine by me.'

'But I do want the money!'

'Right. So, here's the deal. If you are well behaved you can go to the fair. If you help me with the washing today and tomorrow – pegging it out and bringing it in – I will give you an extra £2.50 on top of your pocket money. How does that sound?'

Danielle's eyes lit up. 'Wicked!'

Jonathan and I had already arranged to give Danielle £5.00 pocket money a week, which was a figure set out by Social Services, so if she played her cards right she'd have £7.50 in total for the festival – a sum we considered was sufficient for her to have fun with, without it being too extravagant. I knew Danielle was interested in buying a poster of her favourite pop stars and there are always some small funfair stalls at the festival. Having a bit of extra money in her pocket seemed like a very good goal for Danielle to aim for.

We had a relatively good couple of days, and Danielle

had an excellent trip out with Deirdre, to a local park where there's an outdoor tennis court. They hired racquets and had a knock-about then strolled around the park, visiting a newly built education centre next to the car park. Deirdre told me she thought it would be a good idea to use their sessions not only to keep Danielle's mind busy and to occupy her time, but to help her get fit too. I was delighted to hear that. Danielle was unhealthily overweight and it could only be a good thing for her to slim down.

'We'll support you with this, as much as we can,' I said. 'If she loses weight it will help her self-esteem too, of course, and I think that's something that needs working on.'

'Yes,' Deirdre said. 'I agree, Angela. It's just a question of finding something Danielle likes. It can take time to find the right activity.'

Danielle had enjoyed the tennis but she told me afterwards she didn't want to do it every time she saw Deirdre.

'It was hard work,' she said. 'I was worn out.'

'Well, that's fine, I'm sure,' I said. Deirdre was a very approachable person, and I could see she wanted to do her best by Danielle and achieve positive results. 'You need to just tell Deirdre how you feel. She wants you to have fun and enjoy the sessions.'

Deirdre had told us she had teenage twins who had both gone off to work abroad as au pairs for a year, and that she missed having them at home. 'The plus side is, I can devote more time and energy to my job. I'm making the most of it, and I was very pleased when I was assigned to be your family-aid worker.'

That was music to my ears. It felt like we had a top team around us, and I was confident Deirdre had the skills to help make a difference to Danielle's life.

'What sports have you played before, Danielle?' I asked her, later that day. 'Is there anything you like, in particular?'

'Chase the Ace,' she replied. 'And Snakes.'

'Chase the Ace, the card game?' I asked.

'Yes. He taught me it. He played it at his work. And he let me play Snakes on his phone.'

'He? Who taught you?'

'Him. My dad.'

When she mentioned Chase the Ace my first thought had been to explain that playing cards wasn't really classed as sport, but that would have to wait. Now I was all ears. I had heard nothing about Danielle's family, and if she wanted to talk about it, I wanted to listen and make it as easy as possible for her to tell me whatever she wanted to.

'Your dad taught you?'

'Yes. Ha ha. Bet he plays a lot of that now.'

'He plays a lot now, do you think?'

'Yes. He's got nothing else to do, has he? He won't be able to play Snakes though.'

'He won't?'

'Nah. You're not allowed to have a phone inside, are you?'

'Inside?'

'He's inside, Angela. Prison. Isn't that right?'

She turned to look behind her, seemingly directing her

question at one of the ornaments on the windowsill in our lounge, before turning back round to fix her gaze on me again and painting a big smile on her face. It was a smile that looked completely fake, and I smiled awkwardly back at her.

'Anyway. I'd like to do crazy golf next time. Deirdre said she'd take me to that park over the bridge. Have you ever played crazy golf, Angela? I haven't. It's something I've always wanted to do. I think I could be good at that. I like those little mini castles. I'd like to live in a castle, wouldn't you?'

I had lots of questions in my head, and whether or not I wanted to live in a castle was certainly not one of them, especially not at that moment in time.

Poor Danielle. I hadn't been aware her father was in prison, and I wondered if it had been in the paperwork I'd been given and perhaps I'd missed it? I was sure it hadn't been mentioned, as I would have remembered something like that.

I thought what a terrible thing this was for a young girl to deal with. I wanted to know exactly why her father had been locked up, but of course my priority had to be to make sure Danielle felt able to discuss whatever she wanted to with me. She had to set the agenda, I knew that. So I told her I would love to live in a castle.

'Mind you, there'd be a lot of dusting to do, and it might be a bit chilly,' I mused, before quickly adding, 'Danielle, you know you can talk to me about anything you like.'

She folded her arms tightly in front of her chest. 'But can I *trust* you, Angela?'

'You can trust me. Of course, if you tell me anything I think Social Services have to know, I would have to pass that on to your social worker, Susan. You like Susan though, don't you? We're all here to help you. That's our job. Don't let that put you off. When we share information it's all for your benefit, because we all want the very best for you, and you can trust us all.'

Danielle nodded. 'I like Susan. She's all right. OK. Thanks, Angela.'

That was the end of the conversation. Even though, as ever, it was difficult to follow Danielle's thought pattern and logic, I felt it had been a healthy chat and hoped it might pave the way for more disclosures.

That night Danielle said something intriguing, just before she went to bed.

'You didn't ask me why I'd like to live in a castle, Angela.'

'I didn't, did I? Why would you like to live in a castle, Danielle?'

'Because if a taxi came I could pull up the drawbridge!'

'A taxi?'

I searched Danielle's face for an explanation but she buttoned her lips, threw her head back on the pillow and shut her eyes.

'Night night, Angela.'

'Night night, sweetheart.'

7

'Women are angels and men are horrible'

Danielle was in a great mood when she went to the music festival, proudly clutching her well-earned pocket money in her purse. I'd taken her for a haircut that morning, which I'd had permission from Social Services to do, and she was looking the best I'd seen her. Her dark eyes were clear and shining and she was wearing a new belted dress I'd bought her in town. It made her look a much better shape than she normally did in the long, billowy skirts she often chose, and she put on a neat pair of flat shoes instead of her old trainers for a change. Before she went out I complimented Danielle on her appearance and laid the ground rules out clearly, setting a time for her to come home and agreeing that she would walk back with Shelby, whose big brother would collect her by car from our house afterwards.

Everything went to plan and after the festival the two girls arrived home on time, looking relaxed and happy.

'We've had a great time,' Danielle giggled.

The way she laughed aroused my suspicions, especially

when she and Shelby gave each other a sideways glance and shared a secret smile.

'What did you get up to?' I asked. They looked a bit nonplussed and giggled rather sneakily, so I tried a more subtle approach. 'What was the best bit, girls?'

'Er, the music, of course!' Danielle sniggered.

The doorbell rang and it was Shelby's brother. He only looked to be seventeen or eighteen and seemed very shy.

'Thanks for picking Shelby up,' I said.

'No problem,' he said, flicking his eyes nervously between his sister and the floor while fidgeting and rattling his car keys in his hands.

Shelby bounded out, hurriedly shouting goodbye, and moments later she and her brother were gone in a cloud of rather toxic-looking exhaust fumes from his clapped-out Fiat Panda.

Danielle and I went into the kitchen and I started making a cup of tea. She came right up close to me – too close, as she often did – and asked if she could have a snack.

'Yes, Danielle. Did you have anything to eat at the festival?'

'Yes, chips.'

'Did you get your poster?'

'No. It was £1 on the door. Had chips and lemonade. Bought candyfloss. Then I had no money left. Not a penny!'

I playfully rolled my eyes. I was not going to say anything about all the junk she'd consumed, accepting that's what kids do on occasions like this. Rather, it was Danielle's long-term habits that needed to change, and every day I was making an effort to steer her towards making healthy food choices, at least at home. I didn't keep fizzy drinks in the house and never have, because I've seen them turn some children hyperactive in a flash, or cause them to have sugar rushes and crashes. I limited the number of biscuits and sweet treats I offered to Danielle too, and whenever we had cakes and puddings I tried to stick to home-made recipes that didn't contain large amounts of fats and sugars or hidden additives.

'How about a yoghurt or a bowl of cereal? Maybe a banana?'

Danielle was standing so close to me now that I could smell her breath, and I smelt cigarette smoke, not only on her breath but clinging to her clothes.

'Have you been smoking?' I asked, keeping my tone even.

When a child comes to us and is already smoking Jonathan and I can't stop them, but we always try to guide them in the right direction and encourage them to give up.

'Yes, so what?' She curled her lip and looked me square in the eye.

'Danielle, you're too young to smoke and it's very bad for your health. How did you get the cigarettes?'

'Friend of Shelby. She lives by the bus station. We saw her in town. I only smoked one though.'

'Is this the first time you've smoked?'

'No. I've already got fags and a lighter in my room, if you must know.'

Now her hands were planted on her hips and she was jutting her chin out defiantly in my direction. I found myself feeling uneasy. It was impossible to predict what mood Danielle would be in, and sometimes I barely recognised her as the same girl from one day to the next, or even from one hour or minute to the next.

'Danielle. I would prefer you not to smoke and I won't allow it in or around the house. Your lighter needs to be down here in the kitchen. That's a very strict rule in our home. Can you fetch it for me, please?'

She tut-tutted but, to my surprise, she went straight upstairs and fetched a nearly empty pack of twenty Benson & Hedges and a cheap disposable lighter. Jonathan walked in the kitchen just as Danielle put her stash on the table.

'Oooh,' he said, coolly raising an eyebrow. 'Bad habit. Me and Angela used to smoke, many moons ago.' In a woeful voice, he continued, 'Giving up was the best thing we ever did. Very hard though, wasn't it, Angela? Terrible!'

I immediately tuned in to what Jonathan was trying to do. He wasn't going to reprimand Danielle. He was going to try to talk to her on a more subtle level, giving the impression he was talking to her adult to adult. I figured it was probably the best way forward. I sensed, as Jonathan did, that telling Danielle off about smoking was unlikely to work. Smoking at that age is typically all about wanting to be grown up, so Jonathan's approach was quite clever. The last thing either of us wanted was to give Danielle any excuse or reason to smoke again, and if she thought it would really get to Jonathan and me then she might do it just to cause trouble or rebel or because she liked to do the opposite of what we wanted her to do.

'Get lost! *You two* used to smoke? I don't believe it!'

'Oh yes,' I said. Now it was my turn to adopt a sorrowful tone. 'You see, when we were teenagers it was the sixties and seventies and everybody smoked. Nobody knew how bad it was for you. We all thought it was cool. Can you imagine! And by the time we found out it could give you lots of nasty diseases that could damage your health or even kill you, we were hooked.'

Jonathan nodded sagely. 'That's right. Hooked, we were. Both of us. Such a struggle to stop. Hardest thing ever. Nightmare. If only we'd known at the time how bad it was. Your generation is very lucky, Danielle. You have all the information we never had. So the smart people don't smoke. The clever people never even start, let alone get addicted, like we did.'

She looked at the packet of cigarettes on the table. 'I didn't smoke all of them,' she said. 'They're not even mine.'

'Goodness me!' Jonathan exclaimed. 'I didn't think you had. I can't imagine you'd be so silly. Gosh, no. If they're not yours, who do they belong to?'

'Shelby's friend. The one who, er, lives by the bus station.'

'Right, do you think we should return them to her? I could run you down there, if you like.'

Danielle bit her lip.

'We stole them,' she said, her cheeks flushing red. 'Sorry. We stole them last week from the same girl we took the fags off today.'

She started to sob.

'I'm not worth anything! I'm cheaper than a packet of fags!'

Her sobs turned to a dramatic wail. I wasn't sure if she was putting this on, as it was so over the top, but either way I wanted to make it stop and help Danielle deal with this.

'Can I give you a hug?' I asked.

Danielle threw her arms around me and I felt her hot tears soak into my blouse. 'Take your time, Danielle. Tell us what happened and we'll try to help you put it right.'

Danielle stopped crying as quickly as she'd started and then took on a deadpan expression. It was quite remarkable to see the transformation: I reckon a trained actress would have been hard pushed to have pulled it off so well, although I still wasn't sure if the emotions she displayed were genuine or not.

She confessed that the 'friend' of Shelby was in fact a young woman with special needs. From the description of the girl and where she lived, I realised I knew who this person was. She was called Pippa and she had cerebral palsy, which impaired her mobility and speech. Pippa had been into our shop on many occasions over the years and it was well known she was a target of bullies in the neighbourhood. I was very shocked to discover that Danielle and her friends were now three of her bullies.

Slowly and reluctantly, she explained that the girls had talked about clubbing together to buy some cigarettes on the way to the music festival. Apparently, there were always some teenage boys hanging around near the convenience store, and in return for a fag or two they would go into the

shop and buy cigarettes for anyone underage who was prepared to cut them a deal. However, at the last minute the
girls decided they wanted to keep all of their money for the
festival, and so they came up with a plan to call on Pippa
and steal cigarettes from her instead of buying them. The
three friends knocked on her door, invited themselves into
Pippa's house and said they weren't going away until she
gave them all the cigarettes she had in her house. This,
Danielle admitted, was also how they had got the packet of
Benson & Hedges that was now sitting on our table. Pippa
had given them three cigarettes this evening, and Danielle,
Mina and Shelby had had one each, smoking them at the
music festival.

'Thank you for being truthful,' I said, catching Jonathan's
eye. 'Our number-one concern is for your health and safety,
and you also have to understand it's very wrong to steal, Danielle. It's our job, as your carers, to look after you and keep
you out of danger, whatever danger that might be – whether
it's smoking or going into a stranger's house like this. That is
not OK, under any circumstances. Do you understand?'

Danielle sniffed and nodded her head.

'Now, have a snack and get yourself up to bed. We'll talk
about this again tomorrow.'

'Thanks,' Danielle whispered.

She wolfed down a yoghurt and then stood up and
turned to walk upstairs. As she reached the kitchen doorway my heart sank, because I noticed a large wet patch on
the back of her beige-coloured cotton dress. Then she said
something that made me catch my breath.

'The thing is, women are angels and men are horrible, aren't they, Angela? Isn't that how it is? I wasn't in danger. Don't worry about that. It's OK to go in a stranger's house if it's a woman.'

She darted up the stairs, leaving Jonathan and me looking at each other in dismay and calling after her that we would definitely have a talk tomorrow.

'What did that mean?' Jonathan puzzled.

'And how could she have wet herself like that and carry on as if nothing had happened?' I said. 'Oh my God, she's such a complicated girl. I think we'd need a PhD in psychology to work her out!'

'I know. Sit down,' Jonathan said, scratching his head. 'I'll make us a fresh cuppa.'

He pulled out the chair Danielle had just vacated and gestured towards it, as he wanted me to take the weight off my feet.

'Oh no! What now!' he exclaimed.

'What?'

'Look.'

The upholstered chair was completely soaked through, and this was clearly not the result of Danielle just sitting on the chair in a wet dress. She must have sat down and wet herself while we were there, talking to her as she ate her yoghurt.

Thankfully, we had our appointment with the doctor in two days' time, to discuss a strategy to help Danielle with her incontinence.

'It can't come soon enough,' Jonathan said.

'Quite. I've never known anyone of her age to have a problem like this. It's such a shame.'

Hatty was popping round the next day to meet Jonathan and me, and to take Danielle out to a local farm they had visited together on many occasions over the years. I was very much looking forward to meeting Hatty. I'd found out that as well as being a former headmistress and working as a CAMHS volunteer, Hatty was a local magistrate. I thought what an amazing woman she must be, not only to have kept in touch with Danielle for so many years, but to make time for these day trips.

In the morning, Danielle acted as if nothing had happened the night before, with the smoking and the wetting of the chair. It was like she was in denial, because it must have been obvious we'd discover the soaked-through chair, and that I'd see her wet dress and underwear when I next went to do the washing. However, Danielle seemed in a relaxed and cheerful mood, acting as if she didn't have a care in the world. She told me she was looking forward to seeing Hatty, and I could see she was feeling excited about her day ahead.

I didn't want to upset Danielle's mood, but I had to say something about what had happened with Pippa, at least: I'd told her we'd talk about it this morning and I needed to be true to my word. I kept the discussion to a minimum, reiterating that Jonathan and I wanted to keep Danielle away from any danger and trouble – whether that be damaging her health with cigarettes, getting into trouble with the law for obtaining cigarettes the way she had done or entering a stranger's house.

'I want you to be safe and happy,' I said, 'but what you did yesterday is dangerous in lots of ways. Aside from it being against the law to enter a person's home and force them to hand over something of theirs, it's also morally wrong.'

Danielle interrupted me at this point and looked a bit blank.

'What's morally, exactly?'

'If you behave morally, you behave decently. You are doing the honourable thing, behaving properly. If something is morally wrong, it is dishonest. It goes against decent, honest, reliable and truthful behaviour.'

'Oh.'

I felt I had made my point and I didn't want to go overboard and set Danielle against me. It was becoming clear that a large part of the problem here was that Danielle was still learning the difference between right and wrong, and what was acceptable behaviour and what wasn't. As with the bed-wetting and her personal hygiene problem, I had to try to educate and help her. As we'd already worked out, giving Danielle incentives to improve her behaviour was clearly going to work better than imposing any kind of penalty or sanction, and I had a strong gut instinct that Jonathan and I had to persist with this strategy, however much Danielle was testing our patience.

'You can carry on going out into town with your friends

as long as you don't go to that young lady's house ever again. Is that agreed?'

'Yes.'

'Jonathan and I have lived in this town for many years and the customers who come in the shop are very good at letting us know what's happening. Please don't try to get away with anything behind our backs. We will find out, Danielle. Please follow the rules. They are for your benefit.'

Finally, I explained that I would have to speak to Danielle's social worker about this, to pass on what had happened and to ask Susan's advice about how to deal with it, particularly in terms of making amends with Pippa and recompensing her for what had been taken from her.

'There will be consequences,' I said. 'You do understand that, Danielle, don't you?'

She seemed accepting enough of this and didn't give me any backchat.

'You're a bit like Hatty,' she said thoughtfully. 'I used to try to get her to tell me off but she's like you. She doesn't tell me off.'

I took that as a compliment, and I was now looking forward to meeting Hatty even more, as she clearly knew Danielle extremely well.

When Hatty arrived to collect Danielle I smiled to myself, because she was exactly how I imagined she would be. Dressed immaculately, she was very polite, charming and well spoken.

'Isn't your hanging basket beautiful!' she remarked as

she stood on the doorstep, admiring the display of Creeping Jenny geraniums that Jonathan had worked hard to cultivate.

He grinned like the Cheshire Cat. 'Thank you. I'm very pleased with how the basket has turned out this year.'

Hatty came inside and Danielle appeared genuinely happy to see her. She didn't run up and hug Hatty, but she was smiling with her eyes as well as her lips and I could see she was on her best behaviour, trying to please.

'Where are we going? It's the farm, isn't it? I love the farm! Remember when we had those iced lollies and the horse tried to steal mine?'

'I do! How funny! And do you remember that time you tried to feed a Shetland pony a mint and he whipped the whole packet out of your hand?'

Danielle burst out laughing.

'Oh my God, I'd forgotten about that! He ate the paper and everything. It was scary!'

'Well, not scary enough to put you off the farm,' Hatty smiled. 'I like it there too. I'm looking forward to going back. I heard they have a new petting area. They have lots of rabbits and guinea pigs and you can go into their enclosures and cuddle them.'

'Awesome! Is that true?'

'Totally true. Shall we get going?'

I can't lie, Jonathan and I were looking forward to having a bit of a break from Danielle, and when Hatty said she expected they would be out for around three or four hours we were relieved the trip would not be any shorter. It was hard work looking after Danielle full-time. We'd never cared for a child of her age who wasn't attending school before and always seemed to be under your feet, and we weren't used to it. School holidays are different. Children need the rest, their friends are off too and Jonathan and I always plan holidays and trips out. It's a totally different vibe to having a child out of school in term time.

The work Miss Powell set only took Danielle an hour or so, and she flatly refused to do anything over and above what her tutor asked her to do. I'd asked if it was possible for Miss Powell to give Danielle more homework but was told that, unfortunately, she didn't have time to mark any extra work. All she could do was suggest what Danielle could do herself, but of course she didn't want to do anything she didn't have to, which was frustrating. Danielle's academic age was well below her real age. I didn't have any official confirmation of this, but I could see the work Danielle was doing was for primary children, probably around the Year Four and Year Five mark. I reckoned it was on a par with work an average-ability eight- or nine-year-old child might easily produce.

'I really can't wait to have a proper chat with Hatty,' I said to Jonathan after they headed off. 'She clearly knows Danielle very well indeed. It will be very interesting to hear what she has to say.'

'Fascinating, I reckon,' Jonathan said.

'Yes. That's probably a better word. Fascinating.'

8

'I want to be the good Danielle but sometimes the bad Danielle won't let me'

Danielle was buzzing when she got back from her trip with Hatty, and she told me all about the petting zone at the farm.

'Can we get a guinea pig?' she asked. 'Please!'

I was taken aback by this question. We'd had rabbits and guinea pigs before and we hadn't been planning on getting any more, at least not for the time being, but more to the point, we still had no idea how long Danielle was staying with us. It was unlikely but not impossible Social Services might find her a new school place any day. For all we knew she could be moving out within a week – or she might be with us for months. We really had no idea, and I didn't want to buy pets purportedly for Danielle while we were so unsure of her plans.

'Gosh, do you think Scooter would get jealous?' I said in a light-hearted way, as I didn't want to issue a flat refusal.

If Danielle didn't have Scooter I might have been open to

105

persuasion, even in such uncertain circumstances, as I do believe that having a pet is beneficial to a child in many ways. It teaches them to take responsibility for another living creature, and troubled children often talk to their pets, which is a healthy way for them to verbalise their emotions. Danielle did talk to Scooter and she was fairly good at cleaning out his cage and making sure he was fed and watered, which was always good to see.

Despite her problems, I had started to hope Danielle would be with us for a good while longer. I felt we were making progress – albeit sometimes erratic rather than steady progress – and that I was starting to understand her and learn how to handle her better. I wanted to help Danielle and I really cared about her. It was heartening that she had asked for another pet, because it showed that she was settling in and also that she was not averse to staying with us for a while longer yet.

'Goodness me, I'd forgotten about your hamster,' Hatty remarked. I'd invited her in for a cup of tea when she brought Danielle back from their trip. The two of us hadn't had the opportunity to talk yet, and of course I was hoping Hatty might be able to give me some helpful background information on Danielle. Jonathan was in the shop, and I hoped I could talk to Hatty in private, without Danielle listening in.

'Where is Scooter and how is he doing?' Hatty asked.

'In my bedroom! Do you want to see him?'

'I'd love to, Danielle.'

I suggested to Danielle she could go upstairs and carefully

bring Scooter's cage down to the kitchen. She agreed and ran off, whistling to herself as she did so. When she was out of earshot Hatty quietly asked how things were going. I told her I felt that, on the whole, we were taking positive steps forward despite Danielle being a challenging girl to care for.

'Yes, that's what her first foster carers, the Smiths, always told me. I do hope this time the progress can continue. I can see she's happy here, and she's told me she likes you both.'

'That's very good to hear. Jonathan and I don't really understand what went wrong with her second set of foster carers, by the way. Is there anything you can tell me? All we know is that the placement broke down after Danielle was excluded from school.'

We knew by now that Danielle had been expelled from her last school after damaging another pupil's property and some school equipment. Nelson had told us this, but we had no further details, other than the fact she'd been on a final warning and so there was no other option but to remove her when she caused the damage.

'We were told that once she was at home full-time, the carers who were going to be her "forever family" could no longer cope,' I continued. 'But she was happy there too. In fact she still calls her previous carers her "forever family", and she says she's been in contact with them since moving in with us, although I'm not sure if that is true or not.'

'Ah,' Hatty sighed, looking at me over the edge of her half-moon spectacles. 'I'm afraid I don't fully understand the situation with her previous carers myself – or should I say I don't understand Mr and Mrs Davies – Glennis and Mike as Danielle calls them. They refused to let me see Danielle when she was living with them, and they stopped Danielle from seeing the Smiths, which I found baffling. I was infuriated, to be perfectly honest, as Danielle adored her first carers. She has known them since she was five, and she lived with them for five years.'

I was afraid Danielle was going to reappear at any second, but thankfully I heard the bathroom door closing upstairs and realised she must have gone to the toilet.

Hatty explained that the Smiths were an older couple and that, unfortunately, one of them became ill and they had to stop fostering. 'Danielle called them Granny and Pops. They were marvellous with her and it was such a shame when they had to stop fostering. They had no choice, and it was such a pity for Danielle. I don't understand why she was prevented from staying in touch with them. Such a lovely couple, such a strange thing to have happened. I haven't got to the bottom of it yet, but I'm determined I will.'

Hatty also told me that by the time Danielle left the Smiths' care, they were struggling with her behaviour and constantly asking for support.

Just then we heard Danielle coming down the stairs and crossing the hallway, and Hatty wrapped up the conversation.

'I'm on holiday for a couple of weeks from this weekend but I'll be in touch when I get back, Angela, and we can have another talk. It would be lovely to see Danielle again too. I'll have a think about what we can do next time.'

'What are you talking about?' Danielle asked, appearing at the door with Scooter.

'Do you know,' I said, not untruthfully, 'I was just trying to work out exactly how long you and Hatty have known each other.'

'All my life,' Danielle said.

'Well, not quite!' Hatty chuckled. 'You were four years old when I first met you, Danielle, when you started in the reception class at Hillbank, remember?'

'That's what I mean,' she said.

Danielle had got Scooter out of his cage and was holding him in front of her face, as I'd seen her do on other occasions.

'That's all my life,' she told him, looking in his dark, beady eyes and talking ever so slowly. 'I can't remember anything before.'

Danielle turned her head to look at Hatty. 'Do you want to hold him?'

'Oh yes, I'd love a quick cuddle before I go. Now you take care of Scooter, won't you?'

Danielle nodded and Hatty cradled the pet in her hands, letting him sniff the cuffs of her blouse. She was wearing a sweet-smelling perfume and Scooter didn't seem too impressed: his whiskers were twitching ten to the dozen and he was wriggling around and trying to break free.

'Don't tell Scooter how good you were with the rabbits and guinea pigs at the farm,' Hatty whispered to Danielle, pretending to cover Scooter's ears. 'I think Angela's right, he might get jealous!'

When the day came for me to take Danielle to the GP to discuss her wetting problem she was in a foul mood, but I cut her some slack. I appreciated it must have been embarrassing to have to discuss her bladder issues with someone she'd never met before. The sympathetic doctor I normally took the children to see was on holiday, which was a pity. I had got to know Dr Bates well. Social Services require us to take every child for routine check-ups early on in their placement, to record their weight, size and general health. Dr Bates always had a joke or a kind word to lighten the mood, as he understood that the children we looked after had inevitably gone through a period of change and were still getting used to being in care or living with a new carer.

Unfortunately, the locum on duty on this occasion wasn't cut from the same cloth at all, and he appeared impatient and irritable. He did some routine checks with the air of a man who was bored to tears by his job, and he sighed and spooled through notes on his computer screen as he asked Danielle and me to describe how frequently she wet the bed, and how many times she lost control of her bladder during the daytime.

'It's not every night,' Danielle interrupted defensively, curling her lip. 'And I only wet in the day when I don't have time to go to the toilet or when someone holds me up by talking to me or distracting me. It's so annoying! It's not my fault.'

'It's not every night, but it's most nights,' I clarified, as tactfully as I could. 'And the daytime wetting is not every day. But when it happens, it is quite a lot. What I mean is, Danielle seems to empty her whole bladder. We're not talking about a leak or a small accident that you might not notice.'

'Whatever,' she said impatiently, rolling her eyes. She said this several times, cutting across me as I was trying to talk to the doctor.

The GP sighed again, this time more loudly than before.

'This is a chronic problem and I need to refer you to the incontinence nurse,' he said.

'It's not that terrible!' Danielle snapped, crossing her arms and scowling.

'Chronic means long-lasting, prolonged,' the doctor intoned. 'It doesn't mean terrible. It's a common misconception. I have to explain that to patients all the time.'

I wondered why he didn't change his language if it caused so many misunderstandings, but of course I kept this thought to myself.

The nurse would be able to give 'appropriate counsel' to Danielle, the GP said, rather snootily.

'Appropriate counsel?' Danielle repeated rather too loudly as we made our way out of the surgery. 'What is that supposed to mean?'

'It means the nurse will sort you out. She'll know what's best and she'll help you deal with this.'

'Well, why didn't he just say that instead of trying to be such a clever clogs?'

I suppressed a laugh, as I was thinking exactly the same thing myself. Thankfully, the good news was that the incontinence nurse had a cancellation at the end of the week, so we wouldn't have to wait long for her 'appropriate counsel.'

When we got home Jonathan immediately left Barbara in the shop and came striding into the kitchen to greet us.

'Everything all right?' I asked. I'd expected him to stay in the shop until lunchtime, as we had a lot of orders to take care of and he'd told me he'd be flat out all morning.

'Not really.'

Jonathan walked over to the kitchen worktop and picked up the telephone handset.

'Look at this. What's gone on here?'

The black plastic casing looked like it had been melted. Jonathan clearly didn't know how it had got in that state and I didn't have a clue. We both looked at Danielle.

'What are you looking at *me* for? Why are you blaming *me*? I don't even have my cigarette lighter any more. You made me hand it over. REMEMBER?'

'Who said anything about a cigarette lighter?' I said, raising my eyebrows.

'Look,' Jonathan said. 'Please just tell the truth, Danielle. We can talk about it. We won't shout at you and nothing dreadful is going to happen. But we do need to know what has happened. The phone was fine when I last saw it yesterday and nobody else has been in the house since then, other than Angela and me. This can't have happened by magic.'

'Sorry,' she said, looking genuinely mortified.

I was astonished Danielle had changed her tune so quickly.

'Sorry but . . . I couldn't help it. It wasn't my fault. Someone told me to do it. That's what happened at school, when I burnt that girl's PE kit. It was just the same.'

Jonathan and I looked at each other, and I imagined there was a cartoon-style thought bubble between our heads that said: *So you burnt a girl's PE kit? That's interesting news to us.*

'Who told you to do it, Danielle?' Jonathan asked, staying calm.

'I don't know her name, I forget now.'

'Is it someone you know?'

'Not really. I'm sorry. I shouldn't have listened. Why did I listen?'

Danielle suddenly stared at me with a look of total confusion on her face. I felt tears prick my eyes. She looked so young and vulnerable, and my heart ached for her.

'I'm really, really sorry. Are you going to throw me out?'

'No, Danielle,' I said. 'We're not going to throw you out. We care for you very much and we want to help you. Please go and get me the cigarette lighter or whatever you used to do this.'

She did as I asked, and she also handed over a few cigarettes she told me she had hidden in her bedroom.

'I want to be the good Danielle but sometimes the bad Danielle won't let me. Can I go and have a shower?'

'Didn't you have one earlier?'

'Yes, but I want another one.'

'OK,' I said. 'You can have a shower in a minute, but first we need to talk about this. The number-one issue here is safety, Danielle. It's very dangerous to play with fire. I don't want you or anyone else to get hurt.'

Danielle suddenly talked across me and started asking nonsense questions, as if trying to deliberately annoy me or shut me up, as she had done in the past. This had become a very familiar tactic and, as usual, the questions she asked either made no sense or were misplaced and could easily have waited until later.

'Would you rather eat fire or have knives thrown at you?'

'Danielle, this is important, you need to listen to me . . .'

'I mean, if you worked in a circus, Angela? And what are we eating next Sunday? Is there a roast dinner or can I see my friends?'

'Danielle!' Jonathan said. 'Please listen to Angela. As she says, this is very important.'

She sighed and rolled her eyes but thankfully did stop talking long enough to allow me to continue.

'As I was saying, it's very dangerous to play with fire and I don't want you or anyone else to get hurt. The handset could have burst into flames. Some materials are more flammable than others – and by that I mean can catch alight easier. The phone could have caught fire instead of melting. You could have burnt yourself, and . . .'

'You didn't answer my question! What would *you* do, Jonathan, and what . . .'

'Danielle! You could have burnt yourself, and the last thing we want is for you to get hurt. Do you understand?'

'Oh. Sorry. How could anyone eat fire?'

She started scratching her head and seemed to have lost all focus on the important conversation we were trying to have.

Jonathan took over, supporting what I was saying and giving Danielle a talk about the importance of safety in the home. He wanted to make absolutely sure our message had got through. For a minute or so Danielle seemed to listen and take in everything he said, but then once again she embarked on a nonsensical conversation. This time she stepped right up to Jonathan, forcing him to take a step backwards as she invaded his personal space.

'What would you do if you had no phone, no phone at all?' she asked, staring at Jonathan as if willing him to give the wrong answer.

'I'd talk very loudly!' he said, deciding to go along with Danielle now, and hoping that a bit of humour might help get her on side.

'That's stupid. What if you had to phone someone in Australia or New Zealand?'

'I'd send an email instead. Or a carrier pigeon!'

'That's cheating. I don't trust you.'

She narrowed her eyes and poked Jonathan in the arm. She did this so hard that he was left with no choice but to tell her it was rude to jab like that.

She looked at him blankly.

'What would you do if you had no phone, Danielle?' he asked.

'I'd make YOU buy me a new one.'

'Would you, indeed!'

'Yes, I would.'

She jabbed him again but Jonathan ignored it and instead took another step backwards, asking Danielle to give him some room.

'OK!' she said, backing away. 'But now can we please stop talking about phones? Just because some stupid *girl* made me do that thing, there's no need to keep going on about it, Jonathan!'

He was quite lost for words.

My mum had offered to take Danielle to a production at the small theatre in town one day and I wrapped up this conversation by warning Danielle she would not be allowed to go on the trip if she didn't follow the rules of our house, behave herself and act in a safe and sensible way. This was the last thing I wanted to cancel, as I was looking forward to having some 'us' time with Jonathan, and I really hoped Danielle would pull her socks up.

'Have it your way, then!' she said, and flounced off to have her shower.

We let her go. It seemed like that was the closest we were going to get to her agreeing to toe the line, and we were both feeling pretty worn out. It was tiring just talking to Danielle at times, because you never knew what she was going to say or do next. It had become the norm for Jonathan and me to be constantly on our guard, trying to say and do the right thing in response to whatever Danielle threw our way.

As she made her way upstairs Jonathan whispered to me that he'd never come across anyone quite like Danielle.

'She's so incredibly irritating, but I can't help liking her too. There's something I can't put my finger on.'

'I know what you mean. I think it's when she contradicts herself. It's like something a much younger child might do. It's kind of endearing, which is really quite astonishing, when she's being so incredibly annoying!'

We sat at the kitchen table, the molten handset in front of us, and we both looked at it.

'Do you think Danielle is a fire-starter?' Jonathan asked, taking the words out of my mouth.

It was a reasonable and obvious concern in the circumstances, and we knew from our training that some children found the lure of fire irresistible and could not help themselves when it came to playing with fire. Of course, not only had she melted the phone but she'd also made the alarming remark about burning a girl's PE kit at school. It was very worrying indeed.

'Surely not. We've made our stance very clear on that.'

Jonathan and I had told Social Services that we would not be happy to take in a child who had a history of started fires. It was something we both felt strongly about. We had discussed it at length when the question first came up, many years earlier, and we both agreed wholeheartedly we could not cope with the thought a fire might be started in our home. It was the only condition we had ever set out to Social Services. It was usual for us to have more than one child in the house, and we felt it would not be right to take this kind of risk, not just for ourselves, but for other children too.

'I'm going to call Nelson,' I said.

I looked at the phone receiver on the kitchen table and told Jonathan I would make the call from the extension in the lounge.

'Good. I think that's a very sensible idea, Angela. I'll get back to the shop. There's so much to do and I've really got my work cut out today. We just took on half a dozen new delivery orders, one after the other. I'm not complaining, but I need to crack on or Barbara will be run ragged.'

Nelson was out of the office and I left a message for him to call me back as soon as he could.

'Angela, where's my towel? Where is it? WHERE IS MY TOWEL?'

Danielle was screaming at the top of her voice. I climbed to the top floor of the house as she continued to shout.

'Danielle, please stop shouting,' I called forcefully as I reached the locked bathroom.

'I need a towel, Angela!'

'Is it in your bedroom?'

I wondered if she'd put it back in the ottoman after using it as she'd done before; I hoped not.

'No, it's in here but I can't see it. Where is it?'

'I can't see through doors, Danielle. The bathroom isn't that big – surely you can see it?'

'No. It's steamy. Where is it? Argh! Why is everything so shit? I hate you, Angela. Jonathan is kind but you are so nasty to me.'

I took a clean towel out of the ottoman, placed it outside the bathroom door, told Danielle what I had done and walked downstairs. As I did so I was thinking about that phrase Jonathan had used at the placement meeting. What was it he had said? 'It feels like climbing a mountain and sliding back down just before you get to the top.' How true those words were.

Nelson called back a few hours later. By that time I'd discovered the showerhead was broken in the top-floor bathroom – the one Danielle used. She denied all knowledge of what had happened to it until Jonathan came in from the shop at closing time and asked her exactly the same questions I had.

'Sorry,' she said, fluttering her eyelashes at him. 'I was messing with it. I didn't think it would break.'

'Thank you for being honest,' he said.

'Thank you for being kind,' she said, flicking me a sly glance. 'At least ONE of you is kind.'

When I spoke to Nelson I told him about the melted phone and what Danielle had said about burning a girl's PE kit at school, and asked him directly if she had a history of playing with fire or starting fires.

'Not to my knowledge. I certainly wouldn't have kept that from you. Let me look into it though, just to make absolutely sure I haven't missed anything.'

'Thank you. And is there any other news?'

'You mean in finding a school? Not that I'm aware of,

but I'll check that out too, in case there has been any pro-gress.'

Nelson called me back the following morning to say he could see no mention of fire-starting in Danielle's file, although he advised me to ask Danielle's social worker, Susan, for clarification. 'There's a gap in the dates,' he said, sounding a little perplexed. 'It could be that our records are incomplete or that Danielle was being cared for out of the area for a period of time. Hopefully Susan will be able to tell you more. Unfortunately, there's no news on schools. We still can't find a suitable place for her.'

I called Susan immediately, but she was off on compas-sionate leave for a few days.

'Can anyone else help?' the rather officious-sounding receptionist asked, after informing me that Susan's father had passed away suddenly, following a heart attack.

'I hope so, but I'm not sure.'

I explained that I wanted historical information about a child in our care.

'I see. I'm afraid you will have to wait and speak to Susan. We can't give out confidential information like that over the phone.'

The receptionist's tone was patronising and she really irritated me. I knew full well that Social Services didn't dish out confidential information over the phone and I was not attempting to circumnavigate the rules in any way at all. I just wanted help with a reasonable request for information, from someone in authority who might be able to legiti-mately help me, in Susan's absence. If that meant me going into the office for a meeting or having the information passed to me via Nelson, that would have been fine, but I didn't get the chance to explain this. Nevertheless, I bit my tongue, thanked the receptionist in typically British style and then vented to Jonathan.

'Honestly! What a cheek! One minute she's passing on private information about Susan's father that I didn't ask for, and the next she's reading me the riot act about confidentiality. Some people! I'm going to have to call Nelson back and ask him to get on to this on our behalf. I think he'll be able to make better progress.'

'I agree. But first, cup of tea?' Jonathan raised his eyebrows and gave me a silly look. I'd seen that look so many times, and I knew exactly what it meant: *Calm down, Angela. I know you are just letting off steam. You need to take a breather.*

I kissed him on the cheek.

'I'd love a cuppa. Come on. Let's hope the kettle's intact!'

'Indeed!'

We both chuckled and Jonathan repeated a phrase we've used many times.

'That's the spirit! If we didn't laugh we'd cry!'

9

'Keep your hair on, Angela!'

Out of the blue, I had a phone call from the police, informing me that Danielle was required to go into the local station and give an interview about stealing money, cigarettes and food from a person with learning difficulties. My heart sank. I assumed this person was Pippa again, and I agreed to take Danielle in to be interviewed. After she'd stolen the cigarettes from Pippa the first time, I'd taken Danielle round to Pippa's house and made her apologise to the young woman. I also bought Pippa a packet of cigarettes to replace the stolen ones: this was what Susan advised when I called her to explain what had happened. Pippa had accepted this and the police were not involved on that occasion, which was Pippa's wish, but it seemed Danielle had not learned her lesson and this time had stolen even more from the vulnerable young woman.

When I told Danielle about the phone call and said I was taking her into the police station she froze.

'Will I have to give evidence?' she asked.

Her lips had turned a bluish colour and I realised she was holding her breath. She began to blink rapidly too.

'I can't. I can't do that again!'

'Pippa didn't report you last time,' I said.

'I *know* Pippa didn't report me last time. She could have. Maybe she should have, then this wouldn't have happened!'

Two thoughts crossed my mind. Was the last time Danielle talked to the police about her abuse? Or did she have some other history I didn't know about? After all, we were still waiting for Social Services to confirm she was not a fire-starter.

'Mina and Shelby made me do it! They made me do it!'

Danielle spat out her accusation against her friends and drew in a deep breath. The colour was back in her lips now, and she was looking more animated.

'They made you do it?'

'Yes! I can't believe they've tried to blame this all on me. Shelby was starving and she was dying for a fag. I just went along with it. If I'd had money and stuff I'd have given it to Shelby. I didn't want to go back to Pippa's. I feel sorry for her.'

I told Danielle how important it is to tell the truth to the police, and that she had to think very carefully about what she said in her interview. I also told her I imagined Shelby and Mina would have to give interviews too, which seemed to calm her down a little.

'You have to be one hundred per cent honest,' I said. 'This is serious. You need to tell the truth. Think about it carefully, Danielle. If you don't tell the truth this could get a whole lot worse.'

'OK. Can Jonathan come with us?'

'Yes,' I said. 'He'll drive us to the police station and we'll both wait for you.'

Danielle gave a strange, faraway smile.

'I'm glad about that. Jonathan *always* makes me feel better.'

She gave me a disparaging look as she said this, which made me feel uncomfortable. Danielle had started to make it obvious, almost on a daily basis, that she preferred Jonathan to me. At first I thought she was just trying to wind me up, as she frequently tried to do, but then she had started with the fluttering eyelashes, which hadn't gone unnoticed. Now she was coming out with overt compliments about Jonathan. Obviously, I had to keep an eye on this, because if she had some kind of crush on him things could get very difficult.

All foster carers have to be wary of receiving unwanted attention of this nature, and we all need to avoid situations where we might be vulnerable to false claims of any wrongdoing. In my experience, male carers have to be more careful than female carers in this regard, though other people may not agree. My opinion is based on what I've witnessed for myself over many years, and what I have heard time and time again from other carers as well as social workers, when we attend training and discuss this topic.

On the way to the police station I asked Danielle how she was feeling.

'I don't have to tell you how I'm feeling. You're only a foster carer.'

'You don't have to tell me how you're feeling, Danielle. I'm asking because I care about you and I want to make sure you're OK.'

'Of course I'm OK. I'm innocent. Innocent until proven guilty!'

The interview was very brief. Jonathan and I sat on a couple of extremely uncomfortable wooden chairs while Danielle was taken into a room with two female officers and a third woman, who was an approved 'appropriate adult', as Danielle was under sixteen. Jonathan and I could have attended the interview with her, but she chose to go in with the person recommended by the police. Danielle had a defiant, angry look on her face and she gave each officer and the third female a stony stare as they entered the room.

'I'm glad I'm not going in,' I said to Jonathan.

'Me too. It must be such a tough job interviewing children at the best of times, let alone when they are in a mood like Danielle is.'

While we were waiting outside, a very serious-faced, silver-haired officer walked past and gave us both a look that made me feel uncomfortable. I might have been wrong, but Jonathan agreed that it seemed like the officer was looking down his nose at us, as if it was our fault Danielle was in this situation. I smiled back at him politely, refusing to give him the reaction I felt he wanted: shame or remorse that our daughter, as I imagined he assumed Danielle was, had got herself into this mess.

It emerged that Danielle, Shelby and Mina all blamed each other for the latest theft from Pippa. Shelby and Mina had already been interviewed, and thankfully all three girls were let off with a rap on the knuckles on the understanding they would each go round to Pippa's with a parent or guardian, hand back everything they had taken, replace the chocolates and crisps they had eaten, and apologise profusely to their victim. If there was a repeat of this misbehaviour or the girls got into any further trouble with the law, they were warned the consequences would be much more serious.

To Danielle's horror, Jonathan said he was going to drive straight round to Pippa's from the police station. On the way we picked up plentiful supplies of everything the girls had taken, to pay Pippa back.

'She's going to end up with more than I took in the first place,' Danielle complained.

She didn't notice her slip-up and I didn't pull her up on the fact she said 'I' instead of continuing to blame Shelby and Mina. I did, however, advise Danielle that there would be consequences if she didn't give Pippa a genuine apology, promise never to go near her house again and stick to that pledge faithfully. I added that Danielle also had to pay us back out of her pocket money to cover the cost of the replacement goods for Pippa, which is what had happened last time, on the advice of Social Services.

'What are the other "consequences"?'

'We won't allow you to go into town with your friends if you don't fulfil your side of the bargain and give Pippa a genuine apology that you are going to stick to. We can't allow you out on your own unless we believe your apology is heartfelt and we know you won't repeat this behaviour. Also, you won't be given your pocket money in the first place if you don't behave. You need to earn it with good behaviour. Is that clear?'

Withholding pocket money is generally frowned upon by Social Services and it's not something we ever do lightly, but Jonathan and I both agreed that in this instance it was a tactic that might just work with Danielle, so we were prepared to give it a go. Danielle was such an unusual, intriguing character, and we felt we needed to try things that perhaps we wouldn't have done with a less challenging and perplexing child.

'OK,' Danielle said belligerently. 'It's *clear*. Happy now, Angela?'

'We're both happy to hear that,' Jonathan said, catching my eye. He could see Danielle was trying to cast me as the villain of the piece, and I was grateful for his insight and his support.

Thankfully, when we stood on Pippa's doorstep Danielle did a very good job of convincing Pippa, Jonathan and me that she had learned a lesson, and we felt reassured the young woman would not be bothered again.

'Thanks, Mr and Mrs Hart,' Pippa said as we left. 'I'll still come into your shop. I know it's not your fault and it was all her fault.'

She pointed a finger at Danielle, who looked shocked by this and clearly felt Pippa was being provocative. I steered Danielle hastily away.

'Pippa has some difficulties with how she communicates,' I said to Danielle as we got in the car. 'Don't take that the wrong way. It's done now. Let's all move on.'

I hoped that would be the last word on the matter but Danielle replied, in a deadpan voice, 'I *know* Pippa has difficulties. I can see that. I'm not stupid! But some people have difficulties you can't see so well. Think about THAT, Angela.'

I asked her if she would like to talk about what she meant, but now Danielle had what I'd come to refer to as her 'faraway look' painted on her face, and she stared resolutely out of the car window all the way back to our house, not saying another word.

When we got home Danielle went up to her bedroom and slammed the door. I decided to leave her to her own devices for a little while, but after half an hour my next-door neighbour came to our door, looking awkward and embarrassed.

'What is it?' I asked her. 'Whatever's the matter?'

'Well, Angela. It's – er – I've found wet towels in the garden. I think the girl you have staying with you must have thrown them out of the window or over the fence.'

'Wet towels? Bath towels?'

'No. You know, pads. Sanitary pads. I think they're soaked in urine as they have a strong smell on them.'

'Oh dear,' I said. 'I can't apologise enough. I'll come

round and clear up if you like? And, of course, I'll have words and try to make sure it doesn't happen again.'

'Don't worry about coming round,' my neighbour said, sounding more relieved than anxious now. 'There were only three of them, I think, and I've scooped them up already and put them in the bin. There was also a dry one and that's gone too.'

'I'm terribly sorry you had to do that. Thank you for being so understanding.'

Unexpectedly, my neighbour then gave me a wonderful smile.

'Angela,' she said, 'I think you are incredible. I could never do what you do. I can't imagine what you have to put up with. You must have the patience of a saint.'

I felt myself blush a little. This was a compliment I'd been given many times, but on this occasion it took me completely by surprise and really raised my spirits.

I thought of the male police officer who'd seemed to judge me at the station earlier, and I reminded myself that it really didn't matter what other people thought – especially those not armed with all the facts. It's much better to focus on the positive and realise that, on the whole, many people do understand that being a foster carer is challenging, and that the actions of the children in our care are not necessarily a reflection on how Jonathan and I do our job.

We'd seen the incontinence nurse by now, who was a lovely older lady, very tactful and compassionate and clearly very experienced at her job. Her manner didn't seem to make any difference to Danielle, however, who was uncooperative throughout the appointment. As when we visited the GP, I understood it must have been difficult for Danielle. When she was asked to provide a urine sample, she claimed she couldn't do it.

'There's nothing coming out!' she wailed from behind the toilet door.

I was not surprised about this, as she'd insisted on going to the toilet while we waited for the appointment, even though I said she should hold off in case she had to give a sample. Her response had been, 'Are you trying to make me wet myself? I never know what to do! One minute you're nagging me to go to the toilet and not wet myself, and now you're telling me not to, AN-GE-LA!'

In the end we got her to drink four plastic cups of water and try again, and she managed to produce a small splash that the nurse said was just about sufficient. The sample was needed to rule out any urine infections, and thankfully Danielle didn't have anything in her system that might have affected her ability to control her bladder: in other words, there was no obvious physical reason for Danielle being incontinent, which is what I had assumed, given her history. Her problem was psychological, which was not surprising after the traumatised childhood she'd had.

The nurse gave Danielle some sensible advice about not drinking too many fluids close to bedtime or before she was likely to be in a situation where she couldn't get to a toilet quickly. We were given a spare mattress protector, and Danielle was issued with several packets of large pads, to help keep her dry in bed. If the problem persisted, the nurse said she would look into providing us with a sensor system, which would wake Danielle with an alarm attached to an adult-sized nappy if she wet the bed, to help train her into better habits.

Danielle hated the large pads, and I'm not surprised. The nurse told me privately that sometimes they do the trick purely because girls of Danielle's age are so against wearing them, as they are so bulky it feels very uncomfortable and demeaning, like wearing a nappy.

'I hope that's how it goes with Danielle,' I said. 'It would be brilliant to get her out of this cycle without having to use the alarm and have the full-size nappies.'

Unfortunately, I hadn't banked on what Danielle would do with the pads. Throwing them out of the window was clearly not something I anticipated at all – how could I?

'You're evil!' she had told me when we left the nurse, which perhaps should have given me some warning as to how she was going to respond to the pads. 'How can you expect me to wear those big bulky things? It's so embarrassing. How old do you think I am? And anyway, who says I don't like being wet?'

I didn't rise to it.

'Danielle, this is for your benefit. If you do as the nurse advises, hopefully we can get over this issue and it will soon be a thing of the past. If this doesn't work we can use the alarm, but I think you can do this if you try your best.'

'Hmph!'

Before my neighbour came round I'd already found

wet pads all over the place, unfortunately. When cleaning Danielle's bedroom I'd discovered them hidden under her pillow, stuffed down the back of the radiator and stashed under a pile of clothes on the floor. The bathroom had become another hiding place. The pads turned up in the shower cubicle, at the bottom of the cylindrical container I kept the toilet brush in and lying on the windowsill, sodden through and stinking. She also put them in the ottoman, on top of the clean laundry, which meant I had to rewash it all. Thankfully, I already kept the towels and linen Jonathan and I used in our bedroom, and had done ever since I discovered Danielle putting wet bath towels and soiled clothing in the ottoman. Now, I had taken to packing all the other stored bed linen and towels in clear plastic storage bags to make sure everything stayed clean and dry. This also protected the linen when Danielle put her wet bath and hand towels in there; this had become another of her regular bad habits that she just didn't seem to be able to break, no matter how many times I tackled her and tried to educate her about it.

Throwing the pads out of the window was a new problem, however. Danielle must have hurled them with some force to have scattered them around next-door's garden the way she had. And when she ran out of wet towels she'd obviously decided to hurl an unused one.

I took a deep breath and went to see Danielle in her room.

'Come in,' she huffed when I knocked on the door. 'What is it NOW?'

I explained about the neighbour's visit and Danielle looked crushed and angry, all at the same time.

'You don't understand anything, do you, Angela?'

'You can talk to me, Danielle. I'd like to understand and I'd like to help you. Really, I'm on your side and there's nothing I'd like more than to help you. I'm sure you can sort this out, if you keep trying.'

'You just don't understand. You just don't understand. She doesn't understand, does she?' Danielle was on her feet, padding around her room, directing this question at the walls.

'Angela doesn't know anything.'

'I'd like to understand,' I said. 'I'd like to help you.'

'Well I can't help it, can I? I can't help it when I wet myself.'

She refused to speak about the matter again, and I told her that she needed to dispose of the pads correctly before I'd let her out to youth club again. I would never have penalised her for wetting, but she was old enough to know that it was not acceptable to stash and throw urine-soaked pads around the place as she had been doing.

'OK, OK, keep your hair on, Angela! I'll do what you say. What choice do I have, living in this prison?'

I bit my lip as I tried not to show I was getting annoyed.

By now we'd had several more incidents of Danielle wetting through chairs, and one day she'd also soaked the back seat of the car. Over the last few weeks I'd spent hours cleaning and drying out the upholstery, and as a result I decided to cover one of our living-room chairs discreetly with an absorbent sheet the nurse had given to us. I put a throw over it and also covered the other chairs to match, so as to limit the embarrassment factor for Danielle. I then encouraged her to use that particular seat in the living room, to stop the furniture getting ruined any more.

'I'd like to help you find out why you can't help it,' I said, thinking about what she'd said to me. 'I really would. I want to help.'

'It's not a big deal! I just can't be bothered going to the toilet! You wouldn't, if you were me.'

'If I were you, I'm sure I wouldn't like to feel wet in the day or to have wet clothes and to run the risk of being smelly. I'd want to sort it out.'

'Well bully for you, Angela! You're better than me. You think you are so perfect. I really can't be arsed with you!'

I told her off for being rude and using language like that, but I left it there. I knew there were psychological reasons behind Danielle's problems with wetting and I didn't want to alienate her on the subject or make her shut down completely. She had an appointment with her child psychologist coming up and I was very pleased she was under the care of an expert. I would keep Social Services informed of Danielle's progress with her wetting, and hopefully between us we could help her solve this problem.

If she wins this one, she'll feel so much better, I thought. *She can do it, I know she can. And when she has this victory under her belt, we'll tackle the next problem, and the next.*

I knew by now that any progress we made would not be steady. There would inevitably be setbacks as well as successes, but we'd get there in the end. I was sure of it.

10

'We must be gluttons for punishment!'

When Hatty arrived back from her holiday she arranged to collect Danielle and take her out on another day trip, this time to a wildlife park. When I told Danielle this she punched the air in delight. She'd been on several trips and outings with the family-aid worker, Deirdre, by now and always seemed to be better behaved and in a more responsive mood when she had been kept busy and entertained, and had some physical exercise.

Deirdre had taken Danielle on long walks in the countryside and to the local swimming pool, and she had lost a bit of weight and was looking trimmer and healthier. She seemed happier in her own skin as a result, which was fabulous to see. Her hair was never greasy any more. Instead, she washed it regularly and had begun to experiment with fancy hair clips; she'd acquired quite a collection of pretty hairbands too. It was always great to see Danielle's full face, with her hair pinned back. Her extremely dark eyes looked more exotic than marble-like nowadays and on some days, like today, she had a positive spring in her step.

'I love Hatty!' Danielle declared. Narrowing her eyes, she added, 'It can't be true what they say about her.'

'What *they* say about her?' I repeated back quizzically.

'Glennis and Mike. They hate her.'

I waited, raising my eyebrows and hoping Danielle would continue. Fortunately, she was in a talkative mood and did expand a little after I repeated back, 'They hate her?'

'Yes. The thing is, Hatty didn't like it when they stopped me seeing Granny and Pops.'

'Granny and Pops?'

'They were my first foster carers. I miss them.'

'Ah yes, I've heard about Granny and Pops. I heard they were marvellous.'

Danielle nodded and then told me that she wanted to see them.

'I asked Glennis the other night if it would be all right, now I wasn't living with her and Mike.'

'You asked Glennis?'

'Yes, I called her on my mobile like I did last time, and we had a nice chat. It was when you were in the bath, I think. Jonathan was watching some cricket on the telly. It was boring. You don't mind, do you?' She fixed me with a stare.

This was a tricky question and I didn't have the answer, because I still didn't have a clear picture about exactly what had gone on with Danielle's previous carers.

'What did Glennis say, when you asked about Granny and Pops?' I asked.

'She says it's fine for me to see Granny and Pops now, so that's good.'

'Right,' I said. 'Well I think it would be nice for you to see Granny and Pops too. Leave it with me.'

I couldn't say I was happy about Danielle claiming to have called Glennis again – I had a lot of unanswered questions about her and Mike – and I was relieved when Danielle ended the conversation there. I made a note of what Danielle had said, to pass on to Nelson, just as I had when Hatty spoke on the subject. I didn't know for sure if Danielle had been in touch with Glennis as she claimed, but nevertheless I wanted Nelson to be up to date, and I wanted advice about how to handle this situation.

The next time I spoke to Nelson I filled him in and asked if he had any more information about Glennis and Mike. I knew there was nothing I could do to prevent Danielle from calling them from her own mobile phone if that was what was happening, but still I wanted Nelson's professional opinion on the issue.

'Sorry, Angela, no news on that front yet, but I promise I'll get on to it. I've been making it my priority to look into your concerns about whether Danielle was a fire-starter, and it's good news.'

'Thank heavens for that.'

'Exactly. Danielle is not a fire-starter. There's no history of pyromania or fire-starting or anything of that nature. And just to reassure you, there is nothing missing from her records: it was just a filing error that made me question the inconsistencies with the dates.'

'OK. Thanks. But what about her burning another girl's PE kit? Do you know any more about that?'

'It didn't happen, Angela. I don't know why Danielle said that because it's not true. She was in trouble at school for cutting and ripping another girl's PE kit, which she did more than once, and when she was on a final warning she damaged the school playing field. Danielle was one of a group of girls who let off some fireworks that scorched the field.'

'OK,' I said. 'I'd like to say I'm pleased about that, but it's not that great, is it? And I wonder why she told an unnecessary lie like that?'

'A symptom of attachment disorder, maybe?' Nelson said with a question in his voice. He knew I'd mentioned my concerns about this to Susan, but there had been no feedback from the psychologist as yet, at least none that had been shared with Jonathan and me.

'I went on a course the other day and learned some very interesting things about attachment disorder,' Nelson continued.

He told me he had learned about 'crazy lying,' which was a phrase I'd never come across at that time. He explained that kids with reactive attachment disorder often tell lies that are ridiculously obvious or unnecessary, and they do this because they want to feel in control of a situation, after having felt so out of control when they were being traumatised in their earlier childhood.

'Crazy lying is basically a response to stress,' Nelson said. 'It's very hard to stop a child with attachment disorder lying. All you can do is concentrate on relieving the stress in a child's life, by giving them love and security and so on – all the things you do best.'

'Very interesting,' I said. 'Thank you. I'll look this up. It certainly seems to fit.'

I liked Nelson a lot. Some social workers are so busy and stressed themselves that they don't make time to have conversations like this, but I always find it very helpful to share knowledge and ideas. I think it's essential, in fact, as new research comes out all the time and can be very useful.

'No worries. I think it's fascinating. Hope it helps. I'll be in touch again soon.'

To my surprise, within an hour of me having this conversation with Nelson he called back, with news about Danielle's schooling.

My heart leaped: I was desperate for Danielle to get some proper schooling. The tuition she had with Miss Powell was nowhere near enough for a child her age, and I felt she was missing out on far too much of her education.

'What's happening?' I asked. 'I hope it's good news?'

Nelson explained that, after failing to find a place in a suitable day school, Social Services were now looking at boarding schools. This took me by surprise as I had not even considered boarding school might be an option.

'I've just had a call from Susan. Potentially, would you have Danielle at weekends and holidays, if she were to take up a place as a boarder? There's no need to answer me now, of course, as I know you'll need to think about this and discuss it with Jonathan.'

'Right. I see. I'll talk to Jonathan as soon as he's free. He's just with the accountant, but they should be nearly finished.'

'Thanks, Angela. Fingers crossed. By the sounds of it, this could be the only way Danielle's going to get back into a school environment.'

My gut reaction was that I would certainly be prepared to care for Danielle part-time like this, if that's what it took to get her into school. I realised it would mean Jonathan and I might have to turn down another full-time placement in the future, to accommodate Danielle at weekends and holidays. We were only passed to care for up to three children at any one time, and Danielle would count as a full place even if she were a boarder. This was not a problem though. Danielle's needs came first, and even though I also realised I'd miss having her around full-time – hard work though she was – I felt this could be just the breakthrough Danielle needed.

As I predicted, Jonathan shared my view; he didn't hesitate at all when I told him what Nelson had asked.

'We must be gluttons for punishment!' he joked.

'No doubt about it,' I smiled. 'But seriously, I'm up for the challenge. I feel there's a lot we can do for Danielle, and now we've come this far I want to carry on helping her.'

We'd used the word challenge before, because that was how we viewed Danielle. She wasn't a problem, she was a challenge, and that's a big difference. We felt we could turn things around and she most definitely was not a lost cause.

'Yes, it's the right thing to do, Angela, if that's what's required. She needs as much stability as she can get. We'll do all we can for her.'

Jonathan's words were so true. Danielle had been in care since the age of five. Her father was in prison and she'd lost two sets of foster carers she had wanted to stay with. As for her mother, I had heard no mention of her whatsoever. Danielle's luck had to change, and if we could be part of that process, it would be our pleasure.

On the morning of the trip to the wildlife park with Hatty, Danielle waited excitedly in the kitchen.

'Where is she?' she asked. 'Will she be here soon?'

'She should be here in five minutes.'

'Well what's keeping her? Honestly, some people!'

I laughed. The longer she stayed with us, the more I noticed Danielle had this quirky trait of making herself sound like a disapproving curmudgeon at times. I think she may have been mimicking a character on one of the soaps we watched on TV, but I wasn't sure. I didn't mind it at all: in fact it made me smile, and I found it endearing, as long as she didn't overstep the mark.

'Honestly, Danielle, you are funny sometimes!'

She didn't reply, and her brain seemed to switch into a different mode, provoking behaviour I'd seen many times before. She suddenly started wandering around the kitchen, examining packets, poking her nose into cupboards and drifting into a dialogue that was so nonsensical I realised it would be silly to even attempt to answer her in any logical fashion.

'Why does anyone like this marmalade?' she asked. 'If I had a million pounds I'd buy all the marmalade in the world and throw it in a big lake so nobody could have any more. What would you do, Angela?'

'Well, I like marmalade, actually. I make jams and marmalades sometimes. Mum has a lot of blackberries and gooseberries growing in her garden. At the right time of year, I often make them into jam. Maybe we could all do that together?'

'Gooseberries? Are those the things that look like grapes that have been to the gym?'

I laughed and told her I thought that was a pretty good description, because the gooseberries Mum grew were the large, veined variety.

'You're a clever girl, Danielle,' I said. 'A lot of people wouldn't know what gooseberries looked like, let alone come out with a description like that!'

'Well, Granny used to make gooseberry crumble. She did rhubarb too. She was a bit like your mum, actually. She loved to grow stuff and she was good at baking.'

'Granny as in Granny and Pops, your first foster carers?'

'Yes. What other granny is there?'

Danielle then furrowed her brow and stepped right in front of me, eyeballing me at such close quarters I could feel her breath on my face as she spoke.

'If you had to choose between throwing all the jam in

the world or all the marmalade in the world into a lake, which would you choose, Angela?'

'Neither,' I said, backing away. 'I'd prefer to swim in the lake. Would you like to swim in a lake full of marmalade?'

Danielle looked at me suspiciously. I'd had so many nonsense conversations with her by now that I'd sought advice on the issue from a behaviour expert who gave a timely talk at one of the regular training sessions Jonathan and I attended. The expert taught me the technique I'd just employed: don't bother trying to make sense of it but talk nonsense back instead. She explained that often children who try to reel you into nonsense talks are often simply seeking attention or attachment. If you give them attention in a way that suits you instead of playing their game – which can be infuriating – it's a less frustrating situation.

'Now then, won't it be lovely to see Hatty? Have you been to that wildlife park before? I have. It's one of my favourites. Mind you, Jonathan is not so sure. He got a flat tyre in the car park once and by the time we got it repaired it had started to go dark. We could hear the monkeys calling to each other as night fell. I thought it was quite magical, but Jonathan was a bit spooked, I think!'

'Are you laughing at Jonathan?' Danielle said defensively, taking a step closer to me again. 'Are you taking the mickey?'

'Of course not! I'm just telling you a little story.'

I felt quite exhausted at the end of our strange conversation, and when Hatty turned up to take her out I thought what a relief it was going to be to have some peace and quiet for a few hours.

The trip to the wildlife park was a success, and after dropping Danielle home Hatty promised to ring me at a certain time the following day, when we'd be able to talk in private.

To my surprise, when the phone rang at the agreed time it was not Hatty, but Susan calling.

'Can you come to a review meeting?' she asked.

'Yes, of course, when were you thinking of?'

Susan suggested a couple of dates the following week and we agreed on the first available one, when we'd be able to bring Danielle along too, to take part in some of the meeting. This is normal procedure, so the social workers can ask the child directly how they feel the placement is going, and ask their opinion on possible future plans. Normally the review meeting takes place at six months so this was happening earlier than expected, but I didn't query this: nothing about Danielle's placement had been predictable, and of course we had to discuss the pressing issue of Danielle's education. I was about to ask Susan if a boarding place had indeed been found, but she cut to the chase first.

'I'll get straight to the point, Angela, to give you and Jonathan time to think. There are no schools or boarding schools willing or able to take Danielle. We'd like to discuss whether you would be willing to commit to having Danielle for a further six months, and we'd like to ask Danielle how she would feel about this too. There's a possibility we might be able to get her an extra hour of tutoring, and we'll be able to keep up the contact with Deirdre, the family-aid worker, too.'

'I see. I'll have to discuss this with Jonathan, of course, but my initial reaction is that I feel this is certainly something we can consider, and would like to do. The extra tuition would be helpful, and the support from Deirdre is crucial, but let me talk to Jonathan first.'

Susan said she would pop round and see Danielle before the review meeting.

The phone rang again five minutes later, and this time it was Hatty.

'I really appreciate all you're doing for Danielle,' I told her. 'She had a fantastic day with you yesterday at the wildlife park. I've been hearing all about it.'

'I enjoyed myself too,' Hatty said. 'I think you're doing a remarkable job, Angela. And Danielle clearly adores Jonathan. She did nothing but sing his praises.'

'Yes,' I said. 'I think she's got quite a soft spot for him, to tell the truth.' I trusted Hatty and respected her opinion, and I found myself adding, 'I'm keeping an eye on that, to be honest.'

Hatty listened carefully as I explained how Danielle behaved around Jonathan sometimes. 'It's verging on the flirtatious, on occasion,' I said. 'Jonathan can handle it and is well aware he needs to keep himself safe, but it's not ideal, of course.'

'I see, and I'm sure you know, Angela, it's also important how *you* handle it. I'm not a psychologist, but perhaps Danielle's behaving that way primarily to get to you. I've heard of scenarios like this before and have some experience of them from dealing with other children. It's something to bear in mind, perhaps. If you want to look it up, sometimes it's referred to as "triangulation", when a child puts herself in the triangle and attempts to play one carer or parent off against another.'

This rang true, and I had heard of that term before. In fact, I wondered why I hadn't immediately thought of this myself, and I cast my mind back to a workshop I'd attended a few years earlier that touched on this type of issue.

The trainer had talked about a girl he called a 'Jekyll and Hyde' character, who not only clearly favoured her male carer, but also targeted all of her defiance and abuse exclusively at the female carer. He explained that this might happen when a foster child wants to feel powerful at the expense of one particular adult. Though they probably don't realise why they are doing this, it's likely to be because the child feels weak and lacking in self-confidence. By trying to belittle one of their carers, they are attempting to boost their own sense of self-importance. This typically happens in families where the child can spot that the parents or carers are not in allegiance, though that was most definitely not the case with Jonathan and me. Danielle had expressed frustration several times at how Jonathan and I always had the same reaction or answer, even if we hadn't had a chance to talk to one another. Several children over the years have asked us if we are telepathic, as we never fail to be on the same wavelength when it comes to making decisions about the children in our care.

There was another possible theory that had crossed my mind: Danielle perhaps favoured Jonathan simply because she craved the attention of a father figure. Did she have Jonathan on a pedestal, not in any sexual way, but as an inspirational role model? I shared this latter thought with Hatty.

'That's also a very good thought,' she said. 'You could be right; it would certainly fit, given how she was treated by her own father.'

Hatty had made it clear she was happy to share any information she had that might be useful and helpful, and I was grateful she'd made time for us to talk freely like this.

'We know Danielle was sexually abused,' I said. 'Is there any more you can tell me?'

'Yes, she was abused by her father and also by a group of men known to her father. He and some of his associates are now serving long sentences in prison.'

'I see.' I stuttered the words. It was absolutely devastating to hear this.

'She's a very damaged young lady. The abuse may have started at home from when she was as young as three years old, and didn't come to light until she was five and taken into care. Her mother had abandoned her, and it appears the abuse most probably began when her father was left to bring Danielle up on his own. Then he involved other men, when she was four, I believe.'

'Poor Danielle,' I said. 'It's so heartbreaking to hear this, Hatty.'

'Indeed, absolutely devastating. When I first met Danielle,

she was described to me by a person in a very senior role at Social Services as one of the most damaged children she had ever come across in her thirty-year career. That was about eight years ago, when she first joined my school. Danielle has made some very good progress since then, but of course damage is lasting, in many regards. I think it might be a good idea if you meet the Smiths. They can give you more information than me, and have a lot more experience of looking after her than anyone else. She was with them for about five years, until she was ten.'

'Ten? So what happened in between leaving the Smiths and going to live with Glennis and Mike, earlier this year?'

'Danielle was in a children's home, but that didn't go well. She was so badly behaved that several of the other children threatened to run away if she wasn't removed.'

'Goodness. What a shame she couldn't have stayed with the Smiths.'

It turned out Hatty had been very busy since she returned from her holiday. She'd been in contact with Granny and Pops – aka Iris and Kenneth Smith – and they had expressed their dismay at how they were cut adrift by Glennis and Mike. They also made it very clear to Hatty that they did not want to lose contact with Danielle, and they said they were glad Glennis and Mike were now off the scene. Iris and Kenneth wanted Jonathan and me to get in touch with them, so they could re-establish links with Danielle.

'I still don't know what went wrong with Glennis and Mike,' Hatty said, perhaps pre-empting another of the many questions I had. 'I know the disruption meeting has taken place now, so perhaps Susan might be in a position to shed some more light there. I'm going to speak to her.'

A disruption meeting is a kind of debrief that is held after a placement has broken down. Jonathan and I had never had to attend one so I wasn't entirely sure how much information would come out of it, or how much useful detail, if any, might be shared with us. I made a note of everything I'd heard from Hatty, and the next time I spoke to Nelson I made sure he was fully in the picture too and asked him to keep me updated with any news.

Before this telephone conversation, I'd wondered how Hatty had managed to give Danielle the impressive amount of support she had done for so many years. Hatty was clearly an extremely busy woman, and I was bowled over at how much time and energy she put into her relationship with Danielle, considering she had only been her head teacher for a short period of time, many years earlier, when Danielle was at the start of her primary education. Jonathan and I have kept in touch with many of the children we've cared for over the years and some are just like family now, but even so it's not always easy to find the time to have reunions, let alone to arrange regular day trips and visits as Hatty had done with Danielle for so long.

Now I'd heard how damaged Danielle was, things were starting to make more sense to me. Danielle was a very special little girl, a child who deserved a stalwart of the community like Hatty to go the extra mile for her. The reason behind this – the appalling sexual abuse Danielle had suffered – chilled me to the core.

I asked Hatty if she'd expelled Danielle from her school.

'No, why would you ask that?'

'It's something that Danielle said to me, but I hadn't seen it in the notes so I did wonder if it was true or if she'd got muddled up.'

'No, it's not true at all. She moved so she could attend a school nearer where her foster carers lived at the time.'

At the end of our conversation Hatty gave me a phone number for Iris and Kenneth.

'They're expecting you to call,' Hatty said. 'They're lovely people and they have Danielle's best interests at heart. I have suggested to them that they should also share whatever information they feel may be helpful to you in looking after Danielle.'

11

'I'm glad you're sitting down'

Iris and Kenneth lived in a bungalow on a tidy housing development for the over-sixties. It wasn't quite sheltered accommodation, but there was a duty warden in case of emergency and the complex had clearly been designed with wheelchair access in mind, as in place of steps there were ramps lined with sturdy metal handrails leading to each white-painted front door.

'Come round the back!' a cheerful female voice called when we knocked on the front door.

Jonathan opened the side gate and we went through to the small but extremely pretty garden, where Iris and Kenneth were sitting comfortably on a swing chair. Danielle was out for the afternoon with Deirdre, and we'd fixed up the visit at this time deliberately, so we could talk in private to her first set of foster carers.

'What a beautiful spot!' Jonathan exclaimed as the couple made to stand up. I was thinking the same myself. The garden was a lovely little suntrap, filled with the scent of lavender. 'Oh no, please don't get up!' I said. 'Shall we sit ourselves here?'

I gestured towards a bench in the shade of a tree, next to the swing chair.

'Please do,' Iris said. 'It's lovely to meet you at last.' Kenneth smiled and also said he'd been looking forward to meeting us.

Iris was wearing a floral apron that was fastened tightly around her curvy figure, and she had her grey hair pinned in a loose bun. She looked kind and welcoming; the sort of woman I imagined I could easily sit and chat to for hours on end. Kenneth made a good first impression on me too, looking friendly and very grandad-like. He was dressed in a checked shirt, beige shorts and thick-rimmed tortoise-shell glasses, and, judging from his deep tan and the fact there was an extremely large pair of gardening gloves on the table – big enough for Kenneth's spade-like hands – I reckoned he was a keen gardener.

Jonathan picked up on this too.

'I'm guessing you're green-fingered, Kenneth?' Jonathan said, looking around and remarking on how lovely the roses were.

'Oh yes, I love being out here. Love it!' Kenneth practically sang. 'We struck gold when we got this place.'

'Your garden really is fabulous,' I said, because it was. There were pots brimming with colourful flowers everywhere, and ornamental windmills and wind chimes were blowing in the breeze. The garden felt like a little oasis of calm and contentment, in fact. There were butterflies fluttering around, and bees and insects were creating a friendly buzz in the air.

'He cheats a bit though, don't you, dear?' Iris teased, looking at her husband cheekily.

She then tipped her head towards a particularly eye-popping display of violet and crimson flowers in a window box under their kitchen window.

'Those ones aren't real,' Iris said in a stage whisper.

We all laughed, and Iris told us to make ourselves at home while she fetched a pot of tea.

While his wife was gone Kenneth told us that he and Iris had fostered children for fifteen years. Danielle was the last child they fostered, and they had to give up because of his poor health. Kenneth explained he had a complicated set of age-related problems, including a serious eye condition. 'I won't bore you with the details or we'd be here all day. Terrible thing, getting old!'

He then said that when he was given his last diagnosis, the couple decided it was time to move to the bungalow and stop fostering. 'If things were different we'd have loved to look after Danielle for longer. We love her to pieces. But really, there's no two ways about it. We're past it now. I hate to admit that, but it's true. I know she's better off with a couple of spring lambs like you two!'

Jonathan and I laughed politely. Not only were we both already in our fifties, but also Danielle was proving to be one of the most challenging children we had ever cared for and, in all honesty, we had our doubts about whether or not we were the best carers for the job.

Iris reappeared, setting down a tray lined with a cream-coloured plastic doily and stacked with the tea and a selection of biscuits on a china plate.

'I expect you have a lot of questions,' she said. 'I know I did, when I first got to know Danielle.'

'Yes,' I said. 'Danielle first came to us as an emergency placement a couple of months ago and we've just been asked if she can stay with us for another six months, and we're going to agree to that, aren't we?'

I looked at Jonathan. Even though we knew what a huge challenge it would be, we had both decided we wanted to keep Danielle with us – if she was in agreement, of course.

'Yes. We feel we're making progress with her. She's not the easiest child we've ever looked after though, as I'm sure you two can appreciate.'

Iris nodded and gave an understanding smile.

'I know, bless her. Shall I tell you what we know about her background?'

'Yes please. I think it will be useful, and of course you can talk to us in strict confidence.'

'OK. I'm glad you're sitting down.'

Jonathan and I swapped glances.

I will never forget the conversation that followed. It was like time stood still as Iris spoke in her kind and gentle voice. For all I knew the butterflies were suspended mid-flight, the windmills stopped spinning and the chimes fell silent. That's how it felt: the world itself might have stopped turning. As I listened to what Iris had to say I gasped, sucking in a breath that seemed to have turned to mud in my lungs, because suddenly I couldn't exhale or speak or even move.

'Danielle was sexually abused from a very young age by her father. When she was four years old he started to pass her around a group of paedophiles, in return for money he spent on drugs. Danielle's father was a taxi driver and the men in the paedophile ring were all taxi drivers too. They had a system whereby one abuser would collect her one night and return her later after passing her around. If her father was out at work she had to wait in the garden shed until he came home. Her mother had a breakdown and abandoned Danielle when she was three years old. She appears to have fallen off the face of the earth – never been seen or heard of since. As for Danielle's father, he was eventually jailed when she was nearly seven, along with, I believe, five or six other men. The police operation was huge, which is why it took a long time for the trial to take place. Danielle's father still has many years of his sentence left to serve, although in my opinion it was nowhere near long enough. Danielle's been given a life sentence. He should have had the same.'

Iris paused and shook her head. Then she went on to tell me the month and year when the trial took place, and what Danielle's father was called, in case I wanted to look up old reports from the local paper. I didn't think I could; it would be too distressing, but I appreciated Iris passing on that information. 'It's out there, on public record,' she said.

I thought for a moment and forced myself to speak, though my voice was shaking. 'Danielle said something to me one time about giving evidence,' I said, casting my mind back to when she got into trouble with the police about Pippa. I tried to picture Danielle that day and recall what she said, and I silently remembered the words she had spoken as her lips lost their pink colour and took on a blue tint.

Will I have to give evidence? I can't. I can't do that again!

Obviously, at seven years of age she would not have had to appear in court, but she would still have had to go through the ordeal of telling the police what happened to her. The thought of that saddened me so much. It was heartbreaking, and I wanted to run home and hug Danielle that very minute.

Kenneth dunked a fig biscuit in his cup of tea and now it was his turn to shake his head. After taking a bite of the biscuit and a sip of tea he said, 'When Danielle first came to stay with us she didn't speak, did she, Iris?'

'No, not a word.'

'I tried to get her to talk by playing charades with her,' Kenneth said. 'That might sound odd, but I figured if she wasn't allowed to speak then maybe she might.'

'That sounds perfectly reasonable,' Jonathan said, giving Kenneth a knowing look. 'We've tried a bit of the old reverse psychology ourselves. Did it work for you?'

'Eventually, but not in the way we thought it might. One day, after we'd finished playing and Iris had guessed whatever film it was I was trying to mime, Danielle decided to let rip. "I think you two are cheating!" she accused. She was very hot under the collar. "I think you've done all these old films before! It's not fair! You're mugging me off!'"

Iris chuckled. 'Danielle probably had a point, and we told her as much. I mean, we were doing the old favourites like *Jaws*, I have to admit. Anyhow, we'd have been happy to admit to just about anything if it made Danielle talk. That was all that bothered us. It was a breakthrough, but it was still stop and start for quite some time. Some days she still refused to talk and on other days she wouldn't stop chattering on, talking a lot of nonsense. She also had an imaginary friend who she used to talk to more than us. That went on for quite a while.'

I wondered if this friend still existed, and if this explained why Danielle sometimes lost focus and appeared to be talking to someone else in the room. I guess it was a reasonable explanation, and it's not unheard of for children who have suffered trauma to have an invisible friend, as it's a way they can verbalise their emotions and unload unconditionally, without fear of reprisals.

Iris made sure we all had enough tea and urged us to help ourselves to biscuits before asking if Danielle still had a problem 'staying dry'. I said she did, day and night, and explained all about the incontinence nurse, and the wet pads being stashed all over the place and thrown in next-door's garden.

'I'm sorry to hear that. She was dreadful when she was with us too. She wet herself constantly and she protested wildly every time I tried to get her to wash or to wear dry clothes. Then she told me one day that . . .' Iris looked at

Kenneth, who shook his head again and then looked down at his shoes. 'She said she was used to wearing wet pants, because of what happened with the men in the cars, and she was often in the shed for hours afterwards, always with wet pants. That was her life. It was what she was used to.'

It took me a moment to take in what had just been said. It was one of the most shocking things I'd ever heard. The four of us sat in silence. Iris and Kenneth looked heartbroken and just as shocked as we were: it must have been awful for them to rake up these dreadful memories.

I thought about the children in our extended family, and what they were like at the age of five. Innocent girls and boys with nothing on their minds except what to play with next, which sweets to choose from the shop or how many sleeps it was until Christmas.

I also thought that, from this moment in time, I would never see Danielle in the same way again. What a dreadful, shocking existence she had had. I felt very glad that Jonathan and I had recognised she had complex needs from the start, and tried to reward good behaviour rather than imposing consequences for her 'bad' behaviour. In hindsight, that had been a very good move, because clearly Danielle had had such a traumatic, tragic upbringing she needed understanding and nurturing, not telling off. She had not been taught right from wrong like other children. She had been used and abused by evil men, and she was a very confused and damaged girl. Now, I thought, we'd have to tread even more carefully in how we helped her through each day.

Before Jonathan and I arrived at Iris and Kenneth's bungalow I'd had a mental checklist of questions I wanted to ask, if I felt they were appropriate. After this, everything else paled in importance in my mind. My head ached and I couldn't think what to say, and Jonathan was the same. We subsequently found ourselves, rather bizarrely, making chit-chat with Iris and Kenneth about some random topics like the importance of bees and the shortage of retirement housing in our area, which was a topic I struggled to find anything interesting to say on.

We thanked them both for their help and hospitality and we set up a time to bring Danielle round for a visit: we'd already run this past Social Services and they were happy for it to happen. Iris and Kenneth said they couldn't wait to see Danielle – it had been nearly six months since they'd last seen her – and they paid us a compliment as they bid us goodbye.

'You're two lovely people,' Iris declared. 'I know good hearts when I meet them. Thank God Danielle has finally landed on her feet.'

At that moment I remembered one of my key questions. How could I have forgotten? My mind had been thrown into turmoil.

'Ah, yes, her last carers. I – er – I heard you were denied contact . . . Can I ask, just briefly, what happened with Glennis and Mike? I hope I'm not talking out of turn.'

'That woman!' Iris frowned. 'Least said soonest mended when it comes to that one. I wish Danielle had never stepped foot in that house. Anyway, let's not dwell on the negative. It's a long story and has absolutely nothing to do with Kenneth and me. I want to make that clear. I'll tell you about it another time, if you really need to know. But personally I'd say good riddance to bad hearts. I'm just glad Danielle's out of there.'

It was a lot to take in. As Jonathan and I drove home we began to pick over what had been said.

'It's no wonder at all that senior Social Services officials described Danielle as one of the most damaged children they had ever come across,' I said.

'Poor child,' Jonathan said. 'You think you've heard it all, and then you realise what evil bastards there are in this world.'

Jonathan very rarely swears. I looked at him and saw tears trickle down his cheeks. I put my hand on his knee. 'Come on, love. Like Iris said, best not to dwell on the past. For Danielle's sake we need to look forward, not back.'

We discussed how we could help improve Danielle's life. Making sure she kept up all her various dates with the psychologist, the tutor, Deirdre and Hatty was very important, of course, and Jonathan and I wanted to do everything in our power to change Danielle's life. We wanted to help her put the past behind her, but was that possible?

We talked about what else we could do on a practical level. During her time with us we'd already been asked to take in two other children, just for the odd night of respite care. I'd refused, based on my gut feeling. Now Jonathan and I decided to formalise that decision, and we both agreed that while Danielle was with us we'd give her our full attention and make it a rule not to take in any other children at all, not even for one night. We felt this was a positive step, but still we wanted to do so much more. Really, we wanted to have a magic wand and transform Danielle's life for the better, overnight. We felt so protective of her, and so sorry for her. We desperately hoped that when we had the upcoming review meeting she would be happy to agree to stay with us for the extra six months, so at least we could have the chance of doing as much as we possibly could for her.

The review meeting went well. Danielle immediately said she wanted to stay with us, as long as Scooter could stay too. This made everybody smile, and Nelson made a joke about whether or not Social Services had passed us to care for a 'cheeky rodent' like Scooter. Danielle laughed, and it was so good to see her looking relaxed in such a situation.

I often try to put myself in the child's shoes and remember what I was like at their age, as far as I can. I was the sort of child who didn't like being away from my parents, and those rare occasions when I was forced to spend time away from my mum and dad are still etched on my mind. I hated it, and I couldn't imagine how I would have coped if I'd had to go into foster care or be moved from one carer to another. I also try to remember other times in my life when I've felt like a fish out of water, like when I started primary school and even when I got my first job as a teenager. I was nervous and anxious and I didn't like the feeling that the ground was shifting beneath my feet and my life was changing.

I imagined that being in this review meeting, even for a short time, would be a hundred times more disconcerting for Danielle than anything I had ever experienced as a young person. She must have felt so lost and lonely and unsettled, and so disappointed with the hand she'd been dealt that had brought her to this point. Her dad had betrayed her and he was in prison. Her mum had run out on her, and now she had to face all these people who were deciding what would happen in the next chapter of her life. No child should have to go through what she had suffered, and my heart went out to her, it really did.

Jonathan and I said emphatically that we were more than happy to have Danielle staying with us, and she smiled. As she did so I noticed her shoulders drop by what looked like several inches. She must have been hunched up with tension until that moment, which I found upsetting.

A duty social worker took Danielle to wait outside, and when she'd left the room Jonathan and I told the team we'd met with Iris and Kenneth and were going to reunite them with Danielle, as we'd previously discussed.

'We feel it will be a very positive thing for Danielle to keep in contact with them. Can I ask, have you got to the bottom yet of what happened with her previous carers, when they stopped Danielle seeing Iris and Kenneth, and Hatty?'

'Yes,' Susan said. 'We have.'

She explained that when Glennis and Mike were fostering Danielle, they were questioned about benefit fraud. Apparently the story had recently been on our local news, though Jonathan and I hadn't seen it. I think Susan pointed this out to make it clear she was not breaching confidentialities, as the matter was in the public domain.

'It appears they tried to cut themselves off from people when the police got involved, presumably as they didn't want anyone to know what was going on. Unfortunately this meant cutting Danielle off too, from the people she was closest to.'

'I see,' I said flatly, thinking how incredibly selfish this was, and how unlucky Danielle had been to be caught up in such a situation.

I was extremely annoyed with Glennis and Mike, but relieved Susan had shared this information. At least we'd got to the bottom of the mystery at long last, and I thought to myself that it was hardly any wonder, in the circumstances, that Glennis and Mike could not cope when Danielle was excluded from school. They clearly had enough on their plate already.

Susan's frankness gave me the confidence to explain that Iris and Kenneth had filled us in on the details of Danielle's abuse, and to ask if there was anything else we should know.

'Jonathan and I want to help Danielle as best we can. We don't want to take in any other children while she is with us, so we can focus fully on her needs. If there is any further information that you feel might help us, it would be good to hear that now.'

Susan replied that she felt we were 'up to speed.'

'Danielle's psychologist is pleased with how she is

responding in her sessions. I'll ask her if there are any useful tips she could pass on to you, if you'd like me to?'

'Yes, please, we would. I feel we need all the help we can get.'

It was very disheartening to hear what Danielle had gone through because of Glennis and Mike's problems and I still had a lot of questions I wished I could find answers to. After the meeting I vented some of my anger at the situation.

'How could they let their actions affect Danielle like that?' I fumed to Jonathan. 'And if it's true that they told Danielle we were only looking after her for the money, what a nerve, in the circumstances! Let's hope that part is not true.'

Jonathan let me rant for a while before suggesting, wisely, that there was no point in dwelling on what had happened in the past, as it wouldn't change anything. I had to agree. It was time to move on, in a positive way. Danielle was staying with us and we were determined to turn her misfortunes around and help create a better future for her.

12

'It's your job to worry about kids like me'

Danielle had dropped a dress size thanks to the exercise she was doing with Deirdre and because she was eating a healthier diet most of the time, at least when she was at home with us and we could keep an eye on what she was consuming. I must admit, I told Jonathan I was a bit envious, as I would dearly love to drop a dress size!

We decided to take her to an out-of-town shopping centre to buy her some new clothes, and she seemed thrilled at the prospect.

'I've never been there!' she said. 'I've always wanted to go! Why are you being so nice to me?' She suddenly looked suspicious, and I made sure I nipped this in the bud.

'Danielle, you need some new clothes and that's why we're taking you shopping. There's no hidden agenda!'

'Hidden what?'

'By that I mean there is no hidden reason. You need new clothes, and the out-of-town centre is a great place to go shopping as they have so much choice, and all the shops are big so there's always a good chance you can find what you want.'

'Are you sure?'

'Yes, absolutely certain.'

In fact, Jonathan and I thought it would be a nice treat for her too, and it seemed fitting for Danielle to have a fresh wardrobe when she was starting a new phase of her placement with us. We wanted to do everything we could to make her feel good about herself and to make her happy while she was with us.

Unfortunately, the shopping trip was fraught with tension. Danielle wouldn't trust my opinion on anything and wanted to show everything she tried on to Jonathan for his approval.

'Where is he?' she shouted from the door of the changing rooms in one of the department stores.

'He's gone up to menswear, Danielle.'

'Can you go and get him?'

'No, sweetheart. He's probably trying things on himself. He's after some new shorts. I said we'll meet him in the cafe.'

'Oh! I'll just leave it then!'

She calmed down after we'd had a drink and a snack but then her face fell when Jonathan said he hadn't found what he was looking for and needed to go off on his own again.

'Why can't you stay with us?'

'Because I have things I need to buy, Danielle.' He added in a whisper, 'That's what I always do when Angela is shopping for clothes. I keep out the way, I think it's best!'

Danielle smiled and reluctantly accepted this, agreeing to carry on shopping just with me. It wasn't a pleasant experience at all, because for the next hour or so she insisted on trying things on that didn't fit properly or were inappropriate, then blaming me when they weren't right. If I suggested she might need the next size up or said a different style might suit her better, she snapped at me.

'You don't like anything, do you? How am I supposed to shop with you? It's impossible!'

Eventually I said we'd better call it a day, and that flicked a switch.

'No!' she cried in alarm. 'No, I'm not calling it a day!'

After that she completely changed her attitude and did her very best to find all the items we had on our list. When it was time to meet Jonathan in the car park, Danielle had several carrier bags full of all her new clothes, which included two skirts, a couple of tops, a pair of shorts, new underwear and a sports bra.

As we stepped outside the front entrance of the shopping centre, Danielle spotted Jonathan walking on the opposite side of the car park. All of a sudden, and without any warning, she bolted towards him, completely failing to spot a car coming round the corner. The driver slammed on the brakes and missed hitting Danielle by a whisker: the front of the car stopped so close to her that it actually brushed into her shopping bags. The lady driver got out, looking visibly shaken.

'Are you all right?' she asked in alarm.

'Yes, no thanks to you!' Danielle shouted. 'I think you

need to go and take your test again. You shouldn't be on the road.'

'I'm so sorry,' I intervened, firmly taking hold of Danielle's arm and steering her away. 'I think she's probably in a little bit of shock. I'm really sorry about this. Are *you* all right?'

The lady managed a weak smile. 'Yes,' she said. 'Thankfully no harm has been done. I think you need to teach your daughter some road sense though. She might not be so lucky next time. It's just as well I was going so slowly.'

When we got home Danielle tried on her new clothes and decided to stay in her favourite outfit, which was a blue skirt and cream-coloured top.

'I love this,' she said, giving a little twirl in the kitchen.

'So do I! You look terrific, Danielle. I'm so pleased you got some things you like.'

'Me too. Sorry if I was a bit annoying. I'm not used to shopping. Can I walk to the newsagent's and get my magazine?'

I agreed that she could, and my heart swelled when I saw her striding confidently down the street. This was what I'd hoped for: I wanted Danielle to feel good about herself, and this certainly seemed the way to boost her confidence.

It was just before 4 p.m. when she set out, and when she hadn't returned by 4.30 p.m. I started to wonder where she'd got to. The shop was less than ten minutes away, and she hadn't said she was going anywhere other than straight there and back. Jonathan and I discussed whether he should walk down to the shop and look for her, but then we agreed to wait another ten minutes.

'She was in such a good mood when she went out,' I said. 'I'd hate to spoil that.'

Jonathan agreed. 'She's probably just met one of her friends and got chatting.'

When Danielle hadn't turned up by 4.40 p.m. I sensed something wasn't right. She had left her phone behind so I had no way of contacting her. I dialled the home numbers I had for Shelby and Mina and she wasn't there, though her friends were both out too. Shelby's brother said he thought they might be up on the estate as his sister had said something about meeting her mates up there. I thanked him and hung up.

The estate is a large, sprawling conurbation of council houses on the outskirts of town. As housing estates go, it's not the most pleasant and there are often undesirable characters hanging around. Jonathan said he'd drive up there and see if he could spot Danielle, and in the meantime I called Social Services to let them know she'd gone missing.

'If she's still missing at 9 p.m., call the police,' the duty social worker advised.

'OK. Thank you. Hopefully it won't come to that.'

I made a note of the time of my call and then went through to the flower shop to help Barbara clear away our displays from outside the front.

'Everything all right?' Barbara asked.

She knew me very well and could tell something was on my mind. Also, it was fairly unusual for Jonathan not to help shut the shop up, as there's a lot of lifting involved and pulling down of shutters.

'Oh, the usual, Barbara,' I said. 'Kids!'

I never discussed any details of the children's lives with Barbara and she understood this.

'I don't know how you do it,' she said, giving me a look of admiration. 'I'm glad mine are off my hands now.'

'Barbara, if I had a pound for every time you'd said that to me over the years, I'd have made more money from you than from selling flowers!'

We both chuckled and got on with the job in hand. It was at moments like that when I was very glad to have the shop as a distraction. Just seeing the flowers and being surrounded by their scents never failed to lift my spirits, and it was great to have a loyal ally in Barbara. She truly helped make life easier for Jonathan and me. We could always rely on her to help out when we needed her, even at short notice, and she always had a kind word to say to brighten your day.

Jonathan drove around every street on the estate and saw no sign of Danielle. Then he scoured the town, checking the newsagent's and even going past Pippa's house in case the girls were up to their old tricks. At 6.30 p.m. he went back to the estate and drove around all over again. It was 7 p.m. when he finally spotted Danielle, smoking at a bus stop with Shelby, Mina and a group of boys. As soon as she spotted our car, Danielle quickly passed her cigarette to Shelby, who took it despite already having a cigarette in her other hand.

'I've come to take you home,' Jonathan said, after parking up and winding down the window.

He said nothing about the smoking, but Danielle obviously thought she had to try to defend herself nonetheless.

'Shelby! What are you doing smoking two cigarettes!' she said, completely unconvincingly. 'Are you crazy?'

Shelby looked nonplussed and the boys sniggered. Jonathan rolled his eyes. It was a comical situation in hindsight, but at the time he didn't see the funny side.

'Please get in the car, Danielle. Can I offer you a lift home, Shelby?'

'No, thanks,' she said. 'I'll walk.'

Danielle huffed and puffed as she got in the back of the car, pulling a face at Jonathan and looking at her friends as if to say: 'What a loser this guy is!'

It's a Social Services rule that foster children must sit in the back of the car when travelling with only one adult, for safeguarding reasons. It reduces the risk of the child making a malicious allegation or of simply distracting the driver. We don't always feel it is strictly necessary with every child in our care, but we always stick to the rule, and on this occasion Jonathan was glad to have some physical distance between himself and Danielle. She was in such a negative and manipulative mood, and when she was like that it was very wise to be on your guard.

Jonathan stayed calm on the short journey home and asked Danielle why she had gone missing like that, without letting us know.

'I don't know. No idea,' she said, deadpan. 'What are you going to do about it?'

'Angela and I were both worried. If you'd been gone any longer we'd have had to think about calling the police.'

'So? What are they going to do? Arrest me for meeting my friends?'

'Danielle, there's no need for this attitude. You said you were going to buy a magazine and you've been gone for nearly three hours. If you'd have asked us if you could meet your friends we probably would have allowed it, so why cause all this unnecessary worry?'

'It's your job to worry about kids like me.'

Jonathan had no answer to that; he felt completely exasperated.

'You've missed your dinner too, which wasn't a thoughtful thing to do, was it? Angela made a pasta bake, enough for all of us, as we expected you to be at home for dinner. Have you eaten?'

'No.'

'OK. There's plenty left and you can have it when we get in. Thank goodness you're safe.'

'Do you know what, Jonathan? Anyone would think you were trying to get a part in *EastEnders*, the way you carry on. This is such a huge drama out of nothing. I don't know, I really don't.'

'What if something happened to you and we had no idea where you were?' he said.

'What if nothing happened to me and you had no idea where I was?'

'Look, the point is we need to know where you are. You don't have to stay in the house all the time. There is no need to sneak off. We're happy to let you go out with your friends, but we do need to know where you are.'

When they got home I reiterated what Jonathan had said, staying calm and explaining to Danielle why it was important we knew where she was and what she was doing.

'My God, you two don't half nag all the time. You don't have to repeat what HE said, Angela. I'm not stupid! And I know you don't really care. You're just scared Social Services will stop your money. I know what's really going on!'

I bit my tongue and swallowed my irritation.

'No. We want you to be safe, and we care about you very much.'

Danielle wolfed the pasta bake down at breakneck speed and went up to her room.

'It really does seem that when things are going well, she tries to spoil everything,' Jonathan said, looking forlorn.

'I know. I thought how great she looked when she went out earlier. It's like she's deliberately sabotaged the day; like she pressed the self-destruct button.'

At that moment I heard a retching sound. Jonathan and I both dashed out of the kitchen and into the hallway, just in time to see Danielle throw up, all down the stairs.

'Oh no, you poor love!' I cried.

'Sorry,' she stuttered, her face a chalky white. 'So sorry.'

She retched once more and was sick again. The vomit was splattered on just about every stair and splashed up the wooden banisters. 'Come on, let's get you cleaned up. Oh dear, what a shame. Come on, let's get you to the bath-room.'

I helped Danielle wash her face and encouraged her to clean her teeth while Jonathan fetched a glass of water.

'What have you eaten?'

'Pasta bake.'

'Anything else, while you were out?'

'Can't remember.'

'Well, you need to try. Let's have a think back.'

I listed what I knew she'd eaten that day: a bowl of cereal, a piece of flapjack as a snack at the shopping centre, followed by a jacket potato with tuna and sweetcorn for lunch.

'I went to the kebab shop before, with Shelby.'

'Before Jonathan collected you from the estate?'

'Yes. We went to the new one, by the bookies.'

And what did you have?'

'A kebab, of course.'

'Anything else?'

'Chips. Coke. Oh, and then a packet of Monster Munch. And I finished off Shelby's food, as she was stuffed.'

'Why didn't you tell me you'd already eaten all that when I gave you the pasta bake?'

'I thought you'd go mad and I thought I could eat it. I still had room.'

'Danielle, there is no way I'd have wanted you to eat a meal on top of everything you had when you were out. You should have told me.'

'Sorry. I'm not telepathic like you and Jonathan, you know.'

The following day Danielle had a session with her psychologist.

'Today I'm going to tell her about being raped!' she announced loudly over breakfast. She was tucking heartily into a large bowl of cereal and appeared to have made a full recovery from the night before.

'I see,' I said, carrying on drying the dishes, even though I felt like I'd been kicked in the stomach. Her tone was completely at odds with the content of her shocking statement; she sounded practically upbeat, as if she was going to tell the therapist about a successful day trip or some other triumph. 'You've decided you're going to tell her, your psychologist, about being *raped*?'

'Yes. I'd better tell you first though, I suppose.'

'You can tell me anything you like, Danielle. You know you can always talk to me.'

She began drumming her fingers on the side of her steaming mug of tea.

'It's like this,' she said thoughtfully.

I braced myself, as I was fully expecting Danielle to talk about what had happened in her childhood.

'The reason I didn't come home straight from the newsagent's yesterday afternoon was because a man raped me.'

'Danielle . . . you were raped by a man, when you went to buy your magazine, yesterday?'

'Yes. I thought I'd get into even more trouble if I told you last night, that's why I said nothing. I thought you might think it was my fault. I was worried about what to do, and that's why I went to find my friends, you see. But what happened was—' She stopped in mid-sentence and took a glug of her hot tea. 'Urgh! Can I have the sugar?'

'Yes, here you are.'

'Anyway, what happened was, he grabbed me when I walked past the alley by the newsagent's, and he dragged me behind some bins. Nobody saw. There was nobody around. I was on my own. I thought you better know, before I tell the psychologist. Are you glad I told you, Angela? Are you?'

'He grabbed you, when you walked past the alley by the newsagent's?'

'Yes. He looked like . . .' She screwed up her face and thought very carefully. The description she came out with matched that of a vagrant who was well known in the town.

'Did you tell anyone at all? Your friends? Anyone else?'

'No, I just ran off and found Shelby, because I knew she'd be up on the estate. I knew she was meeting the boys.'

Danielle's words just didn't ring true. I couldn't put my finger on exactly why, but I really wasn't sure I believed her. It was just a gut feeling I had: something wasn't right about this. If she'd been raped, surely she would have been in a terrible state, not in the mood to stand at a bus stop, smoking with her friends? But then again, I knew that traumatised children like Danielle were so used to switching off their emotions, it became second nature. Maybe because of what happened to her as a child, she was able to pull the emotional shutters down even on an event as dreadful and disturbing as a rape?

I asked several more questions, being careful to stick to what Danielle had already said and not put words in her mouth or lead her to say anything she didn't mean.

'Will you need to call Social Services?'

'Yes. And the police will need to be informed.'

As soon as I said this Danielle started to clam up. I wasn't sure if it was because she wasn't telling the truth or because of her past experiences. I told myself to be very careful not to let Danielle see I had any doubts. I needed to show her I was on her side, and was there to help her.

'You mustn't worry about Social Services or the police. They are there to help you, just as I am. I'll help you with this, Danielle.'

'I want to talk to my psychologist,' she said, sounding robotic. 'I can't talk any more to you. Can we just leave it?'

She went upstairs to brush her teeth, walking like a zombie as she did so. My brain was working ten to the dozen as I tried to process everything Danielle had said and work out how best to take things from here. I wanted to call Social Services and the police immediately, as they would need to interview her as soon as possible and gather any evidence they could.

Danielle reappeared minutes later, and as she came down the stairs and reached the hallway the support worker who was taking her to her session with the psychologist was already knocking at the front door.

'See you later, Angela,' Danielle said flatly, opening the

door. 'Sorry for all the hassle. Just forget what I said. I bet you wish I'd never darkened your doorstep.'

'Don't say that, Danielle! That's not true at all. Are you sure you feel up to your session today?'

I was stalling for time, knowing I couldn't just let her go without talking to the support worker at least.

'Yes, I want to go. I'll be fine afterwards. It will all go away. She told me it will be fine.'

I wanted to ask who 'she' was but there was no time. I thought perhaps she meant the psychologist and was just a bit muddled, but I wasn't sure.

Danielle had already put her shoes on and stepped out of the house. I let her walk to the car, and as she did so I asked the support worker if I could have a word.

'Of course. What is it?'

'Danielle has just made a very serious allegation,' I said, quickly explaining what she had described. 'She clearly wants to go to her session today, but I want to put in a phone call to the office and discuss this before you take her.'

'That's very wise. I'll wait in the car with her, shall I? I've got a new CD. I'll distract her with that.'

'Perfect. Thanks. Hopefully this won't take long.'

I called Social Services and was put through to a senior social worker straight away. He told me he would take things from here and that I should let Danielle go to her session with the psychologist. My job was to pass on the facts as I'd been told them; I'd learned that lesson very early on in my fostering career. All you can do as a foster carer is report what you have seen or heard. It's not our role to express opinions or speculate; we can only deal in facts and it's up to other professionals to carry out the relevant investigations.

I was relieved Danielle was going to see the psychologist. It seemed like good timing and I felt the therapy session could be very helpful indeed, whether Danielle was telling the truth or not.

Jonathan had been out at the wholesaler's that morning and when he returned later on and I filled him in with what had happened, he had a similar reaction to mine. He was shocked and saddened but his instincts told him he was not entirely sure Danielle was being truthful. Jonathan commented that her description of being dragged into an alley seemed a little clichéd, and he said it was odd that she'd gone to eat a kebab and so on afterwards.

'Also, that description she's given. That's the homeless guy who's normally at the coach station, isn't it?'

'Yes, that's what I thought, straight away. He fits the description perfectly, and he always wears that distinctive coat she has described.'

'Well, as it happens I saw him when I was driving around looking for Danielle. He was at the coach station, in his normal spot. I noticed him because he had a plaster cast on his foot and I wondered what he'd done. What time did Danielle say this happened?'

'She didn't, but I assume she meant when she first went to the shop, which was around 4 p.m., wasn't it?'

'Yes. Well, I suppose it was a good hour later when I saw him up at the coach station. Plus she was sick when she got

home . . . Oh my God, I don't know what to think or believe.'
Jonathan stopped talking and sighed.

'Look, it's not our job to make a judgement on this, is it?
All we can do is support Danielle and do what we have to
do.'

'Quite, but I hope to goodness it isn't true. It doesn't
bear thinking about, after all she's been through.'

Nelson called to tell me Susan would fix up a meeting
with Danielle as soon as possible, and that the police had
already been contacted.

'Is there anything at all you need me to do?'

'Just keep hold of any potential evidence, clothes and
suchlike.'

I'd already washed all of the clothes Danielle had been
wearing the night before. As she'd been sick, I'd put absolutely everything she had on straight in to soak. Danielle
herself had made sure this happened, as she was worried
about ruining her brand-new skirt and top. She'd also had
a shower before bed, and again this morning. I'd taken the
clothes out of soak and put the washing machine on first
thing, and now Danielle's clothes were churning in the
tumble dryer, because it was raining outside so I couldn't
peg them on the washing line.

I looked at the drizzle on the kitchen window and sank
into a chair, feeling as miserable and grey as the weather.

13

'I think we're all doing well. We're on a roll!'

Thankfully, the 'rape' episode was soon over. Danielle confessed to her social worker, Susan, that she invented the story, but not before the police had started to investigate and Shelby and Mina had each had visits from two police officers. The girls were not happy, because neither of them had been where they were supposed to be that evening, and had subsequently got into trouble with their families, who also did not welcome having the police at their doors unnecessarily.

Unfortunately, the girls' friendship never really recovered after that. Danielle flatly refused to discuss with me why she made the false claim, but she did say it was 'all sorted' after her subsequent session with her psychologist, which was brought forward. There was no remorse or explanation, and the only time she ever mentioned it again, she was very defensive.

'You don't need to worry about me, Angela. I'm not a crackpot! It was her that made me say it.'

'It was her? She made you say it?'

'Don't you have a stupid idea in your head sometimes? Like there's a crazy mad person in your head telling you what to do or say?'

'I think we all have daft thoughts and ideas, Danielle. But I don't have anyone *telling* me what to say.'

'Oh no, nor do I. I'm not crackers, you know that, don't you?'

'I don't think you're crackers, Danielle.'

She beamed and I thought silently to myself, *It's a wonder you're functioning as well as you are, given all you've been through.*

Susan told me she had talked to Danielle about the impact on the unfortunate homeless man she had falsely accused of rape. It turned out he had a sound alibi: he was captured on CCTV at the coach station during the time of the alleged attack, and so fortunately he was spared the ordeal of having to defend himself against the spurious allegation.

One day, when I saw an opportunity, I reiterated to Danielle how terrible it must have been for the man to have had a lie told about him. I was trying to teach her the importance of telling the truth and considering the feelings of others, but she didn't seem to take this on board at all.

'What's he got to lose? He's a tramp. He's the lowest of the low. Nobody would believe him anyway, it's just as well he was on CCTV! He got lucky. I never got that lucky!'

'You never got that lucky?'

'No. Nobody believed me, did they?'

She was looking up to the ceiling and appeared to have zoned out. That was the end of the conversation. I made a note of Danielle's comments and reported them to Nelson, who duly recorded it in his Social Services file.

'When she was little, do you think she was told nobody would believe her and she was the lowest of the low?' I said to Jonathan that night.

'It's entirely possible,' he said, shaking his head.

As soon as we knew Danielle was staying with us for at least another six months we had asked her if she'd like to enrol in a club or society. This is something we encourage every child to do who is living with us for more than respite or short-term care.

'Archery,' she said straight away. 'Can I do that?'

'Gosh, I've never come across an archery club before, but I can certainly look into it. Do you have any other ideas, in case that doesn't work out?'

'Judo. Or curling. Or ice hockey.'

I realised she'd watched a TV programme the night before about the Olympics, which focused on some of the more unusual sports.

'Right,' I said, thinking judo was the most likely club to be available on our doorstep. 'Let me make a few calls.'

As I expected, there were no archery, curling or ice hockey clubs in our town, but there was a judo class held in the hall of one of the local schools on a mid-week evening. When I told Danielle she could go for a taster lesson to see if she liked it she cheered.

'Yes! I've always wanted to learn how to have proper fights!'

'It's not exactly fighting, Danielle. Judo is a martial art.'

'Same thing.'

'No, it really isn't.'

'Whatever!'

When the mobile library pulled up in the next street later that day I shot over to see if they had a book about judo. Luckily they had two, so I borrowed them both.

'Have a look at these,' I said. 'That way you'll be well prepared before your class. And you can learn a bit about the history of judo as a martial art.'

'Thanks!' she beamed. 'You're the best, Angela! I'd never fight you.'

'I should hope not,' Jonathan said, having just walked into the room on the tail end of the conversation.

'You mean it wouldn't be good if I knocked Angela out?' Danielle said in a teasing tone, looking at Jonathan.

'Certainly not,' he replied, widening his eyes in mock horror. 'How could you even *say* such a thing?'

We all gave a little laugh, but to be truthful I didn't find the chat very amusing. Even though Danielle spoke in a jokey way, she had a steely glint in her eye, at least when she looked at me.

'Did you spot that?' I asked Jonathan later.

'No,' he said. 'Honestly, I thought she was just in a silly mood, saying things in the nonsense kind of way she does sometimes.'

We still had an issue with Danielle treating Jonathan

and me differently. She definitely favoured him, and I had begun to suspect she fancied him. She craved his approval and attention, and at times she actively sought to cause trouble between Jonathan and me, though she didn't ever succeed. We'd started to make a point of telling her things about ourselves, such as how long we'd been together and what our wedding was like back in the seventies, so she could be in no doubt about the strength of our relationship and commitment to each other.

'Don't you get bored of each other?' she asked me one day.

'No, of course not! We'd be lost without each other.'

'What if one of you met someone else? Would your heart break?'

'Yes, but neither of us have any intention of going off with somebody else. We love each other very much.'

'Urgh! That's gross! If I were Jonathan I'd get fed up of living with a bossy boots!'

'Excuse me!' I said, trying to laugh this off and nip the conversation in the bud before it turned into anything more uncomfortable.

For a welcome month or so we at last entered something of a 'honeymoon period' with Danielle. As I've said before, this usually happens at the very start of a placement, when a child is settling in and doesn't yet feel comfortable enough to rock the boat. We hadn't enjoyed the luxury of this when Danielle first moved in, but now she knew she was with us for a lengthier stay she finally seemed to be calmer and better behaved than before, and it was heartening to see.

For example, my mother went with her to the cinema most weeks because they liked the same kind of films, and she never failed to come back enthusing about Danielle being a 'delight' and a 'pleasure to be with'. The judo classes were a roaring success too. Danielle couldn't wait to get there every week, and she made some new friends who she started to go to a different youth club with. This was very good news, as Shelby and Mina soon disappeared off the scene completely after the rape episode.

Even the bed-wetting got better, eventually. When Danielle didn't make progress with the pads, the nurse gave her an alarm system to use in bed at night, as promised, which was ultimately more effective. This meant Danielle had to wear what was effectively an adult nappy attached to the alarm, and it rang out whenever she wet herself. She went through a phase of switching off the alarm then going back to sleep instead of going to the toilet, and subsequently wetting the bed. This was followed by a frustrating week or so when she disconnected the alarm before she went to bed, so it was neither use nor ornament. Finally, after I talked to her many times about how the system was designed to help her, not hinder her, she started to see the benefit and use the alarm properly.

I praised Danielle every time she was dry, and I said that if she kept up the good work I would buy her a holdall she wanted for judo, with the club logo on the side. It was expensive and quite a luxury to have, as Danielle had plenty of bags she could use for judo, but it seemed to work as a good incentive. When she'd been dry at night for two whole weeks I bought her the holdall, complete with a new water bottle that fitted in a pouch in the side pocket. She reacted as if it was Christmas morning.

'Angela, this is the best present I've ever had!'

'Really? I'm so pleased.'

The next day, when she came back from a trip to the swimming baths with Deirdre, Danielle handed me a small box of chocolates.

'Gosh, what's this for?' I said. 'And how did you know these were my favourites?'

'It's to say thanks for being kind. And I didn't know they were your favourites. But I do know you like *all* chocolates, don't you?'

'That's true enough!' I laughed. By now Danielle was well aware that I lived in a constant state of watching my weight and either being on a diet or feeling guilty that I wasn't.

'We'll open those tonight, when *EastEnders* is on.'

'Yes!' Danielle cheered. 'You're ace, Angela.'

She continued to have occasional accidents in the daytime and the odd slip-up at night, but on the whole fantastic progress had been made and I was very pleased for her.

Danielle's tuition gradually increased and she now had a total of three sessions at a new centre out of town, with a different tutor, Mrs Blake, who was older and more experienced than

Miss Powell. Mrs Blake seemed to get more out of Danielle than Miss Powell, and Danielle would come home chatting about all the things her new tutor had said. She also seemed very keen to please Mrs Blake, which was a good sign.

'I'd like to be clever like Mrs Blake,' Danielle said one day.

'You are a clever girl, Danielle. We all have our talents. You have a great imagination, for one thing. And you know a lot about films, and martial arts.'

For her latest homework Danielle had done a piece of writing about her judo classes, and it was really quite impressive. She'd copied out lots of facts from the library books I'd borrowed for her, and she'd done some super illustrations. Danielle's writing was still very juvenile for her age, in terms of content as well as style and appearance, but nevertheless I could see she was making progress and she deserved praise for that.

'I don't know what job I'm going to do when I'm grown up,' she said one day. 'I don't know what I'm going to be really good at. Did you always want to be a foster carer, Angela?'

'No, but it was something I was interested in from when I was a young girl, because I knew a family who fostered when I was little, and I wished that we could foster too.'

'Why didn't you?'

'My mum and dad used to run the flower shop, and Mum said she wasn't cut out for fostering and didn't have the required patience.'

'That's not true! Your mum would have been brilliant!'

'I think so too, but the shop was harder to run in the old days, before we had computers and the choice of suppliers and delivery systems we have today. Mum was always working flat out and had to put in much longer hours than I do. She was always tired at the end of the day, and as a result she didn't really have the patience she has today. I'd say she was pretty stressed out a lot of the time.'

Danielle seemed fascinated to hear this.

'Thelma? Stressed out? Ha ha, I can't imagine that. She's always so calm and everything. Wow. So how *did* you get into fostering?'

'Well, I began when I was in my thirties. Before that I'd worked for a bank for a long time, ever since I left school. Then, when Jonathan and I took the florist over from my mum, I saw an advert and it got me thinking about fostering again. I answered the advert, Jonathan was happy to do it with me and, well, the rest is history!'

'Did you do it because you didn't have your own kids?'

'No. When we started fostering we hoped we would have children, but it just didn't happen that way.'

'Is that because Jonathan is a Jaffa?'

'A Jaffa? What do you mean?'

'He's seedless.'

She said this with great seriousness. I wanted to laugh but of course I couldn't.

'Oh my goodness, I've never heard that one before. Actually, I wouldn't use that expression if I were you, Danielle; it's not very kind, and besides, there are lots of reasons couples can't have children. Like I said, it just didn't happen for us.'

'Oh. Are you sad about that?'

'No. I consider myself very lucky. I love being a foster carer, and who knows if I'd have carried on if I did have a family of my own? I think things happen for a reason.'

'That's scary.'

'Scary?'

'Yes, because bad things happen, and what's the reason? Tell me that, Angela.'

'You make a very good point, Danielle. I suppose a better way of putting it would be to say that I think we all have to make the most of what life throws at us. We can't predict the future and we can't control everything that happens to us, but the important thing is to look at life in a positive way, and look for the good in things, rather than have regrets.'

'I like that,' she smiled. 'You're very clever, Angela.'

Fitting in all of Danielle's classes and commitments had become quite a task, especially as she was now doing an average of three sessions a week with the family-aid worker, Deirdre, too. However, I wasn't complaining. As far as I could see Danielle had never been happier, and she clearly benefitted from having a packed timetable to follow as her behaviour was so much better than it had been when she had more time on her hands.

The fact that Danielle was seeing Deirdre more regularly brought me an unexpected bonus. Deirdre had started to stay for a cup of tea or a chat with me whenever she had time, and we became friends as well as colleagues. In all my years as a foster carer I've never shared confidential information about a child or the job of a carer with my friends or any members of my family, including Mum. It's not ethical, and in any case I've always thought it was unnecessary, having Jonathan by my side. I felt I didn't need anyone else to chat to about my role and the children in my care, because Jonathan and I unload on each other all the time, and we truly share the job of caring for every child who stays with us. We have a great partnership, and without my husband's support I am sure I would have stopped fostering years ago.

When Deirdre started to become a friend I realised what a help it was to have a fresh pair of ears listening to my worries and concerns, and how useful it was to share ideas and thoughts with a fellow professional who had a very good understanding of our situation. Support social workers like Nelson also perform this role to a certain extent, but by now Deirdre knew Danielle far better than any of the social workers. She spent an average of twelve hours a week with Danielle, one-to-one, and their relationship had become quite tight-knit. Deirdre completely got it when I asked her advice or reported a mystifying conversation I'd had with Danielle. She never told me what to do, but she guided me and offered words of encouragement, and ultimately gave me faith that I was doing my best by Danielle, which was what mattered most.

*

On her thirteenth birthday I threw a little party at the house for Danielle. She invited three of her new friends, my mum came over, Deirdre turned up for a short while and Iris and Kenneth popped in too. Danielle had seen her 'Granny and Pops' a few times by now. On the first occasion Jonathan and I took her over to their bungalow and we all had tea and cakes, and after that I dropped Danielle off so she could enjoy a short visit on her own, which Social Services fully supported.

'Granny and Pops!' Danielle always shouted, running up and hugging them both. Iris and Kenneth were marvellous with her, doing jigsaws, playing board games and always showing a genuine interest in everything she was doing. Whenever Danielle stepped into their living room – which was just as colourful and inviting as their garden – I noticed that she seemed to revert to being several years younger than she was, taking on a very childlike way of playing and completely losing herself in the games and puzzles. There was never any tension with Danielle when she was in Iris and Kenneth's company, and she was always polite and respectful. It was a joy to see her like that.

Granny and Pops arrived at the party carrying two large, shiny pink balloons in the shape of a '13', and the way Danielle reacted was heart-stopping.

'Arghhhh! Wow! Thank you SOOOOO much! You are both LEGENDS! They are the best balloons I've ever seen! Thank you, Granny and Pops!'

'Steady on,' Kenneth chortled. 'Anyone would think we'd given you the Crown Jewels.'

'These are better than the Crown Jewels. What even *are* the Crown Jewels?'

My mother, a proud and staunch Royalist, took up the reigns on this one and told Danielle all about the collection at the Tower of London.

'I'd love to see all those sparkling diamonds,' Danielle said, eyes widening. I made a mental note of this. A trip to London would be another great incentive when the time was right and I wanted to encourage her in some way.

Jonathan and I took Danielle on an enjoyable long weekend break to a mobile home park in the next county, although we did have one or two hiccups. One afternoon Danielle got 'lost' when she went into an arcade. We panicked for a few minutes when we couldn't see her, but the drama was quickly over. She'd decided to give us the slip so she could have one last go on a particular machine.

'Danielle, there was no need to have done that. If you'd have just told us you wanted another go we probably would have let you.'

'Oh! Sometimes I forget I don't have to tell lies! Can we have pizza tonight?'

'Yes, we can have pizza tonight.'

On the last afternoon it rained heavily and I said we'd have to change our plans. We had wanted to visit an outdoor activity centre where Danielle had been looking forward to trying open-air rock climbing but I said we'd have to choose an indoor activity instead.

'I can't imagine the rock-climbing wall will even be open in this weather,' I commented.

'Well you would say that, wouldn't you!' Danielle said sulkily. 'Jonathan wouldn't be so B-O-O-O-RING!'

'Actually,' Jonathan said, 'I think it would be dangerous to climb in this torrential rain. I wouldn't want you to have an accident, Danielle, and nor would Angela.'

'Oh,' she said, looking bemused. 'I thought *she* was just being mean to me.'

'No. We're both focused on your safety, Danielle. Angela is the same as me. She wants the best for you. Now then, how about bowling?'

'Yes!' she smiled. 'Good idea. Sorry.'

We had plenty of conversations like this now. Danielle would set off on a negative track and we would manage to steer her back to a much more positive place.

'Well done you,' I whispered to Jonathan later, when Danielle was about to bowl at the alley and he and I were sitting behind the little scoreboard we had all typed our names into, so the electronic system could automatically record our scores.

'I think we're *all* doing well. We're on a roll!'

As Jonathan said this we both looked up to see Danielle's bowling ball clatter into the centre of the skittles, knocking the whole lot over and prompting the word 'STRIKE' to flash up in bright red on the big screen above the lanes.

'How about that!' Jonathan whooped. 'Very well done, Danielle!'

It really did feel like we were all winning, and I felt so proud and happy that night as we drove home. Danielle snoozed on the back seat of the car and when I looked at her I was filled with a sense of wellbeing. In that moment I believed I could change her life, I really did. She was on track, and it was such a relief to see her like that.

14

'You don't know anything about me, Angela'

Ten days after our weekend break, Danielle went on a boat trip with Deirdre. The weather was pleasant and they drove out to a local beauty spot where you can hire various small crafts or go on a short pleasure cruise up and down the river. Danielle was really looking forward to going on the cruise, and she was in good spirits when they set out. Deirdre bought their tickets at the nearby tourist information office and chatted to Danielle about the different types of birds and wildlife that inhabited that part of the river. She was all ears, drinking in the sights and sounds around her.

'This is like paradise,' Danielle commented as they walked along the riverbank to the boarding point.

They got on the boat and found there were only a few other passengers taking the trip that day.

'This is good,' Danielle said. 'There's plenty of room. What are we going to eat?'

They always had a bite to eat together, and Deirdre told Danielle she was taking her to the cafe afterwards, which was next door to the boat museum, a five-minute walk from the information point. 'We'll have a look in the museum too, if we have time.'

'Wicked!'

When the boat set off Danielle's mood started to change for no apparent reason.

'I'm thirsty!' she said with a threatening tone in her voice. 'Can I get a drink?'

There was a small kiosk on board selling tea, coffee and fizzy drinks.

'I've got some cartons of orange juice in my bag,' Deirdre said.

'I don't want orange. I want one of those bottles of pop. I want the blue one.'

Danielle then started kicking the backs of her heels into the base of the wooden bench seat they were sitting on, prompting the other passengers to look over disapprovingly.

'Danielle, please don't do that. You're making a noise and you might damage the seat. Have some orange juice. It's your favourite brand, the one you like best.'

'No. I'm not having that, you tight cow!'

A couple of elderly female passengers looked horrified, but Deirdre smiled back at them with confidence, refusing to buckle. She was very used to being in situations like this, and her years of experience had taught her not to crumple with embarrassment when a child creates a scene of this nature. She was doing her job as best she could, and if she allowed herself to be bothered by the sideways looks of other people it would not help matters.

'Danielle, please don't be rude. That's not a kind thing to say, and it's untrue.'

'Cow. Tight cow. You're as bad as Angela. I'm gonna kill her one of these days.'

'Danielle, please stop behaving and talking this way. Let's enjoy the trip. Please don't spoil it. And I know you don't mean that about Angela.'

Deirdre began reading a leaflet about the boat museum, thinking the best tactic might be to ignore Danielle. She figured that if she engaged with her any further when she was making such rude and shocking remarks, it might only pour petrol on the flames.

Deirdre's plan worked for a short while. Danielle harrumphed and moved to another seat, and stayed quiet for a few minutes.

'I need the toilet,' she suddenly announced. 'I need it NOW!'

There was a sign pointing to the toilets behind the kiosk about ten metres away, and Deirdre told her to follow it. Danielle did as she was told, but as she walked off Deirdre saw that she'd already wet herself. The back of her trousers was damp, the vinyl seat cover she had been sitting on was sheened with a film of what must have been urine and she also left behind a nasty smell when she walked off.

Deirdre whipped a wet wipe out of her bag, moved next to the wet patch and discreetly cleaned it away. When Danielle returned from the toilet she was acting even more strangely, walking in a lopsided way and gnawing on her hand. Deirdre was watching the clock, desperately wishing for the trip to be over as quickly as possible, but they were only ten minutes into the thirty-minute cruise. Then she noticed that Danielle was watching something too – a bearded and tattooed man who was sitting beside the skipper. This man had checked the tickets when they got on the boat.

'Danielle, it's not good to stare,' Deirdre said quietly, because she was looking at the man so intently and Deirdre was worried about her causing offence.

Danielle didn't respond. Instead she sat as still as a statue, yet her breathing was loud and laboured.

'Danielle, are you all right?'

There was no response at all, and Deirdre said afterwards it was as if Danielle was in a trance. The expression on her face was one of fear, loathing and incredulity. The man she was staring at was in his forties, overweight and scruffy. He had a few teeth missing and, amongst his many tattoos, he had the word 'love' inked on the knuckles of one hand and 'hate' on the other. It crossed Deirdre's mind that this man might look like one of Danielle's abusers, or at least someone she knew who she had reason to dislike, distrust or be afraid of.

At the end of the trip Deirdre had to guide Danielle off the boat; her eyes were glazed and she seemed completely unfocused and disconnected from her surroundings. There was an awkward step to navigate to cross from the boat to the jetty, and Danielle stumbled. As she did so a bottle of blue pop fell to the ground, coming from under her jacket. It was the pop Danielle had wanted from the kiosk. Deirdre swiftly picked it up, wondering how on earth Danielle had managed to get it without her noticing. She decided to tackle that issue later.

They went to the cafe and Danielle said she needed the toilet again. She was gone for what seemed to be rather too long, so Deirdre went to investigate. When she walked into the ladies' toilets she was shocked and dismayed to see Danielle throwing up in one of the washbasins. On the side of the basin was a bottle of liquid handwash with the spout removed.

'Danielle! Oh my goodness, what's going on?'

'I drank it,' Danielle gasped. 'I want to kill myself.'

When I heard the full story later I shed a tear. Danielle was taken to A & E as a precaution. Mercifully she had only ingested a very small amount of the handwash product and, after a couple of basic tests, she was discharged. Jonathan and I picked her up, and on the way home she said she was sorry and that she didn't know what came over her. She also admitted stealing the pop from the boat kiosk when she went to the toilet. She would not say why she had done either of those things, and once she was back home she started to repeat, 'I want to kill myself. I might as well die.'

'Is there anything at all you would like to talk about? I want to help you. You know you can talk to me about anything.'

'No, Angela. I don't want to talk about it. If you don't

want me here I will understand. I can sleep in the shed if you like.'

'The shed? Goodness me, of course you don't need to sleep in the shed. We do want you here. We want to help you. We are here for you.'

A senior social worker came to the house to see Danielle, and a doctor visited, who prescribed a low dose of a common sedative. Jonathan and I were not very happy about this as Danielle was only thirteen and she seemed completely zombified already. Perhaps not surprisingly, the tablet knocked her out, putting her into a very deep sleep. This worried me and I didn't like to see her like that, but we had to trust the doctor, who felt this was the best course of action for the time being.

'It will help her have a good night's sleep and she will hopefully feel a lot better tomorrow,' he said.

Danielle's next session with her psychologist was going to be brought forward and, in the meantime, Jonathan and I were advised to double-check the safety precautions we had in place at home. I did a full swoop of the house, making absolutely sure no chemicals of any kind were within reach. As I expected, anything and everything remotely dangerous was locked away; this is something that's second nature to us after having this advice drummed into us time and time again on foster training courses. Similarly, as I've said before, we never have potentially dangerous items like lighters, matches or sharp objects lying around either. Even Jonathan's tool shed is always kept under lock and key, and he's very vigilant about never leaving it unattended when he needs to open it up to get the lawnmower out or use something from his toolbox.

Despite our home being as safe as possible, when Jonathan and I climbed into bed that night my mind was working overtime. I kept thinking of all the things Danielle might still find that she could drink or try to harm herself with.

'What if she really is determined to kill herself?' I said to Jonathan. 'There are probably all sorts of things she could do. But we can't run the house as if it's a high-security prison, can we?'

'I know, Angela, but I don't think she really wanted to kill herself. It was a cry for help, wasn't it? She only swallowed a very small amount of that stuff. If she meant it, she'd have downed the whole bottle, or chosen something that was properly poisonous.'

I barely slept. Every time I heard a creak in the house I imagined Danielle was tiptoeing down the stairs to search for something she could use to harm herself. The knives in our cutlery set are deliberately blunt and the sharp kitchen knives are kept in a locked cupboard. But what about the pizza cutter or the cheese grater? I remembered that time she said something odd about Scooter, when I was cutting the carrots for him. What was it she said? *He might get a knife and stab you!*

I had to tell myself to calm down. This was ridiculous. Danielle had had a bad day and things would get better tomorrow. But what if she drank all the shampoo and handwash in all the bathrooms? Or ate the toothpaste or swallowed the sun cream that was on the windowsill in the kitchen? The possibilities and risks suddenly seemed endless.

'Are you awake?' I said to Jonathan.

'No,' he said sarcastically, but kindly.

'What do you think triggered it? The man on the boat who Deirdre described? Or something else, something that sparked a bad memory?'

'I don't know. Hopefully she will tell one of us.'

'I'd better let Hatty know. Oh God, Danielle's supposed to have tuition tomorrow. What do you think?'

'Angela, we'll work it out tomorrow. You need to get some sleep.'

'You're right. Night. Sleep well.'

I stared at the ceiling and thought about Danielle lying in her bed upstairs, knocked out with pills. How would she feel when she woke up tomorrow? Would we be able to get through this? I had really thought I could help her turn her life around, and now I wasn't so sure. The abuse she'd suffered had been so horrific. Was she beyond help? Was she always going to suffer relapses like this? Was there any hope she could grow into a normal, happy adult and lead a fulfilling, productive life, away from her demons?

I left Danielle sleeping until 9.30 a.m. the next morning and then I tapped on her door and went into her bedroom.

'Hi,' she said groggily. 'I'm sorry. I don't know what happened. What did happen?'

'It's OK, love. You're safe here. How are you feeling?'

'Tired. But OK, I think. My head aches a bit. Can I have some water?'

'I've brought you a glass. Here you are. Can I sit down?'

She nodded and I perched myself on the edge of her bed. I noticed her eye twitch. It was like a nervous tic and I thought it must have been driving her mad because it refused to go away, although she didn't seem to notice.

'My dad used to smoke drugs,' she said. 'Did you know that?'

'No. I didn't know that. He smoked drugs, did he?'

'He said if I behaved myself, when I was bigger he'd let me have some. You don't know anything about me, Angela.'

A sheen of sweat appeared on her brow. She took a large gulp of water and then shot out of bed and darted to the bathroom.

'I'm going to be sick,' she said, but when she retched over the toilet bowl nothing came out.

She went back to bed, and after a short while I told her I needed to go downstairs and that I would check on her in ten minutes. I'd promised I'd call Nelson to give him an update on Danielle.

'Good morning, Nelson,' I said as brightly as I could manage, but Nelson sounded hesitant and a little anxious.

'Oh, hi, Angela. Er, how are you all this morning? Yes, I'm glad you've called . . .'

I could tell he had something to tell me, something he was worried about saying.

'The thing is, we've decided it would be a good idea if

Danielle went into respite care for a few days, to give you and Jonathan a break.'

My heart sank and I felt my throat constrict.

'I see. When are you thinking?'

'If she is up for it, in terms of being able to get herself up and dressed, we can arrange to have her collected this afternoon.'

'Right. Do you not think the disruption might have a negative effect?'

'We've had a meeting with senior social workers and the feeling is that this will be best for everyone. Danielle is a complex case and this is absolutely no reflection on you and Jonathan. All being well, a spell in respite care will be all Danielle needs. It will help all of you, and hopefully then the placement will be able to resume in a more positive way.'

I felt like a failure and I was so upset. We'd never had a child removed in this way before, and I couldn't remember the last time I'd had no children living under our roof. This was awful.

'You mustn't look at it negatively,' Jonathan said. 'Social Services are giving us all a break, because they hope it will help us carry on, and help us to best care for Danielle in the future.'

I wasn't convinced. I felt a bit naive for having thought I could turn Danielle's life around so quickly. Look what had happened to her! Maybe I wouldn't be able to help turn her life around at all. She was in a worse state than when she arrived with us.

I spoke to Hatty and Deirdre; they both reiterated what Jonathan had said and were very supportive.

'We all need help sometimes,' Hatty said. 'The wise thing is to recognise that and accept it.'

'Thanks, Hatty. You always know exactly what to say.'

'I only speak the truth, Angela. Trust in your abilities. You're doing a great job, and you will do an even better job in the future, I'm sure.'

15

'What's she done now?'

'Let's make the most of the break,' Jonathan said. 'What shall we do tonight? It's Friday, after all.'

'I'm not bothered about going out. I've got loads to do in the house this afternoon and I'm already feeling shattered. Shall we just get a takeaway and watch a film?'

'Great idea. Chinese? And what d'you fancy watching? How about *The Devil Wears Prada*?'

'Chinese sounds good to me. I don't mind what we watch. You choose.'

We'd treated ourselves to a couple of new DVDs as there had been an offer on in our local supermarket, and I knew Jonathan was itching to watch *Casino Royale*, even though we'd seen it at the cinema when it first came out.

'Let's go for *The Devil Wears Prada*,' he said. 'We could do with a bit of a laugh.'

I smiled. Jonathan was so kind and thoughtful, and he was really doing his best to cheer me up. The house felt very strange without any children in it, and I'd got so used to

Danielle being around I kept half expecting her to spring up in front of me, yell for a towel or bang on the bathroom door when I went to the toilet.

I wanted to give Danielle's bedroom a good clean while she was away, and I'd promised her I'd give Scooter's cage a freshen up too, and change his straw.

'You'd better do a good job,' Danielle had said when she left. 'If he's dead when I get back, I swear I'll kill you, Angela!'

She laughed and raised her fist. 'You mark my words,' she said, pretending to square up to me. 'You'd better take good care of him or there'll be BIG TROUBLE!'

'You know you can take him with you, if you like.'

'Nah, he can stay here. It's only a couple of nights. Not worth it.'

Danielle was very accepting of the fact she was having a two-night stay in respite care, with a family she'd never met before, on the other side of town. We were told the carers she was staying with had two teenagers of their own, and Danielle cheekily commented that she thought it would probably be 'more fun in their house than yours.'

'I hope you're right,' I said. 'I hope you do have fun. Now, remember your manners and try to be on best behaviour. I know you can do it. We'll see you on Sunday. I'll do a roast for when you get back. My mum's coming over so we can play some games afterwards if you like. What do you think?'

'Wicked,' she said, albeit rather flatly.

*

209

When I opened Danielle's bedroom door later that morning an overpowering stench of urine hit me. It was so strong it made my eyes sting and I walked straight to the window and opened it as wide as I could, to air the room out. Her bed was soaked and she hadn't bothered to strip it, and her wet pyjamas were lying on the carpet.

I pulled on my rubber gloves, stripped the bed and put all the rest of the dirty laundry I could find into a pile by the door, ready to wash. There were clothes strewn everywhere, and as I tidied up I discovered several sodden pads stashed randomly around the room. One pad was on top of a hair-brush on the dressing table, with a wet skirt on top of it; another was on the bookshelf, seeping its contents onto a collection of well-thumbed Roald Dahl books.

In one corner of the room I found what looked at first glance like a pile of tatty blue ribbons. I didn't recognise them, but when I bent down to have a closer look I realised this was – or had been – one of my favourite blouses. This gave me such a shock I actually gasped and put my hand over my mouth. The blouse had gone missing a few weeks earlier, after it had been in the wash. I'd searched every-where, and I couldn't work out how it had got lost in between the washing line and the ironing pile.

I cast my mind back: Danielle had helped me bring in the washing that day, and she had been in a very bad mood. She dropped several items on the grass and trod on them, seemingly deliberately, so I had to rewash them. I'd told her off, and then she'd had a go at winding Jonathan up, switch-ing the electric lawnmower off from the socket inside the utility room while he was on the other side of the garden. I always keep the ironing in the utility room, and now it was looking very much like Danielle had taken my blouse that day, hidden it in her room and, for reasons best known to herself, decided to cut it up. How she'd got hold of scissors I had no idea, unless she'd bought a pair with her pocket money or taken them from a friend's house.

I felt so deflated, and then I made another worrying find: a cup filled with what looked like a mixture of several different toiletries. There was definitely some orange blossom hand cream in there as I could smell it, and I guessed some of my nail polish remover might be in there too. This was another thing I'd lost recently, and when I looked in Danielle's bin I found the empty bottle. I had a very bad feeling about this mixture. I know lots of kids like to muck about with 'potions'; I've seen plenty of girls trying to make their own perfume or mix up some 'medicine' for their dolls. But given what Danielle had done with the handwash on the trip with Deirdre, I couldn't help looking on the black side. Why had she put the mixture in a cup? Had she been *planning* to drink it, was she just trying to alarm me and use this as another cry for help or had she actually consumed some of it, but not enough to make her ill?

I made a note of all of this, for myself and for Social Services. *What a nightmare*, I thought. I wondered if we'd even be able to carry on looking after Danielle if she was so badly behaved and manipulative, and so apparently determined to derail her own life.

I got a text message as I was heading downstairs with the large pile of stinking washing.

> Can I come and see u tonite? Got new girlfriend.
> Wd like u 2 meet. Jonny X

Jonny was a boy who'd stayed with us for several stints of respite care in the past. His family had a lot of problems, and when he was coming up for sixteen they lost their home. Jonny's parents and little sister ended up in a B & B, while he came to us for a month or so until Social Services found him accommodation of his own.

> Yes. Be lovely to see you. What time?

He suggested 8 p.m.

'That all right with you, Jonathan?' I asked, after popping into the shop.

Barbara was there, so I didn't discuss what I'd found in Danielle's room. That would have to wait.

'Yes, it will be lovely to see Jonny. But what a pity. Perhaps I won't get to see *The Devil Wears Prada* after all!'

'Ha ha. Pity, that, isn't it?' I said sarcastically. 'There's always tomorrow night!'

I hoped the visit would cheer us up, as we certainly needed it. Jonathan had been as shocked and disheartened as I was when I told him about my blouse and the state of Danielle's room. It spoilt our Chinese meal because I told him everything while we ate, as it was the first chance I got that day. It was the last thing either of us needed at the end of a busy day.

Happily, we did indeed brighten up when Jonny arrived. It was great to see him, and his girlfriend was very sweet and clearly besotted with him. Jonathan and I were delighted to hear that Jonny had got himself on to a good apprenticeship, and he had a flat in one of the better blocks of 'halfway house' council housing for teenagers on the outskirts of town. He also told us his family had been rehoused and were 'doin' good'.

'Don't know 'ow they stuck it in that 'orrible B & B,' he commented. 'I was lucky I could come 'ere. You an' Jonathan ain't 'alf 'elped me out over the years. I'll pay yer back one day. Don't know 'ow, but I make that a promise!'

'There's no need for that, Jonny,' I smiled. 'It's just great to see you.'

Jonathan nodded. 'This is all the payback we need. It's brilliant to see you looking so well, and to hear how you're getting on. We really appreciate the visit.'

We meant every word. It was a real tonic, and a very timely one too.

The next morning the phone rang, very early. I reached for it in a half-awake daze, wondering who was calling at this time and what had happened.

'Angela?'

'Danielle?'

I glanced at the clock: it was just after 5 a.m.

'Are you OK?'

'Yes. I mean no. I'm missing you.'

'Sweetheart, we're missing you too.'

There was silence on the other end of the phone.

'Er, what did you do yesterday?' I asked, sitting myself up.

'Played on the Xbox with Jamie and Harry.'

'Jamie and Harry?'

'They live here. They're the real kids, not a fake kid like me.'

I was more awake now and I suspected Danielle was playing the sympathy card. As much as I felt sorry for her, I knew it wouldn't help matters if I played along, and so I skirted over this 'fake kid' remark.

'Are you getting on well with the boys?'

'Yes, kind of. I think Harry fancies me, and he's cute. He tried to kiss me.'

'He tried to kiss you? Did you want him to kiss you?'

'Dunno really.'

'Well don't do anything you're not happy with, Danielle. Do you hear? You do not have to kiss anybody you don't want to kiss. It's up to you to decide. How old is Harry?'

'Same age as me.'

'OK.'

'What are you making for lunch tomorrow, Angela?'

'Roast beef. Mum's doing a rhubarb pie.'

'I think Harry's dad makes Harry's mum foster kids for the money, you know.'

'So you're OK?' I said, again trying to avoid being sucked into an unhelpful conversation.

'Yes, I'd just rather be at home with you and Jonathan. I

know you only look after me because you care. I'm looking forward to coming back.'

'Me too. We do care, very much. We'll see you tomorrow.'

Jonathan was wide awake now and had managed to hear most of the conversation, as I held the phone between us.

'I swear she's like two entirely different people,' he said, rubbing his eyes. 'When she's like this, you wouldn't recognise her as the same girl we've been dealing with at times, would you?'

'Not really,' I said. 'It's like she plays different characters when she chooses, isn't it?'

'Yes, that's exactly right. And I suppose that's not so surprising, when you think of it. I mean, if I'd had the start she had, I think I'd try to reinvent myself.' Jonathan yawned. 'Should we say anything to Social Services, about Harry?'

'I don't think so. It's Saturday morning and it's hardly an emergency, is it? He's only thirteen, and there's nothing wrong with a boy fancying a girl, is there?'

The phone rang again.

'Hello, Danielle.'

'Hello, Angela. Can I speak to Jonathan?'

'No, sweetheart, it's very early in the morning and we're both trying to get some sleep.'

'But I miss him.'

'You'll see both of us tomorrow. Now I think you should try to have a bit more sleep. I'm going to hang up now, and I look forward to seeing you tomorrow.'

'OK. But I just want to ask you something.'

'What?'

'What about Scooter?'

'Scooter is fine. I cleaned out his cage. You'll see tomorrow. Have a good day. Bye, Danielle.'

I hung up.

'I was hoping for a lie-in!' Jonathan said. 'If that rings again, I think we should ignore it, don't you?'

As he spoke my mobile beeped, signalling I had a text message.

Night night X

I sent the same message back and switched off my phone, and then of course I couldn't get back to sleep. I lay in bed thinking about whether this weekend would help turn things around. I wanted to help switch on Danielle's new life. I wanted her to have a fantastic future, but could she? Jonathan was right. She was the girl with two lives – and which one would she take into adulthood? What was it she had said? *I want to be the good Danielle but sometimes the bad Danielle won't let me.* I wanted to be optimistic and I tried to tell myself good would prevail. She needed help and support and a lot of care and love, and if she got that, then the good Danielle would win the day, surely?

Danielle was in a very odd mood when she returned to our house on the Sunday. She rushed up to Jonathan and me with a huge smile on her face, telling us how pleased she was to be back.

216

'Is all my stuff still in my room?'

'Yes, of course,' I said.

I was thinking that I'd have to pick my moment to talk to her about my blouse and everything I'd had to clean up in her room. Now certainly wasn't the time; she needed to settle back in first.

'Are you sure you're not messing with me, Angela?'

'Of course not! Of course your stuff is in your room.'

'I've heard it all before,' she said, jutting out her chin and shaking her head.

I let that go; I didn't know what it was all about.

'Can I help you with anything for the lunch?'

Suddenly Danielle was being extremely pleasant and helpful. It was like a switch had just been flicked in her brain.

'Yes, that would be great. Can you lay the table? There will be four of us, with Mum.'

'No, I don't want to do that. Can I cook something?'

'How about you lay the table first, and then you can help me make the Yorkshire puddings?'

'OK, if you insist. If it's not one thing it's another!'

She took a handful of cutlery into the dining room and then I heard her say an exaggerated, 'Oops!', as she'd done on several other occasions, typically when she was seeking attention. It took me back to when she first arrived and 'accidentally on purpose' – as I believe – smashed her cereal bowl on the floor.

'Everything all right?' I called through, keeping an even tone in my voice.

'Well, not exactly.'

She said this in a weird, faraway voice – exactly the kind of voice you'd put on if you were trying to spook someone.

I thought, *Honestly, what's she done now?*

I went through to the dining room, half expecting to see the knives and forks scattered across the floor or the salt spilt on the table. The sight that greeted me was far worse, and not one I'd anticipated at all. It took my breath away. Danielle was ashen-faced and standing statue-still, holding out her left arm with her palm facing upwards. On the inside of her wrist were four thin trails of blood, all in a neat line. In Danielle's right hand was my large roasting fork. It was the sharpest fork I owned, and when we weren't having a roast I always kept it in the locked cupboard with the cooking knives.

'Oh my God, Danielle!' I said. 'What's happened here?'

I grabbed a napkin from the dresser and blotted away the blood. Danielle continued to stand rooted to the spot, with her arm held out in front of her.

'Sorry,' she said, dead-eyed. 'It wasn't my fault. She made me.'

'Who made you?'

'She did.'

Danielle's performance would not have looked out of place in a creepy horror film. She was in a zombified, trance-like state, and fresh blood was oozing from the inside of her wrist.

'Let's get you cleaned up properly, come on.'

I took the roasting fork off her very carefully and put it

on the table, and then Danielle let me lead her to the downstairs toilet, where I washed her arm. I then told her to sit down on the closed toilet seat.

'I'm going to get the first-aid kit,' I said. 'Stay there.'

I had a first-aid kit in the kitchen so I was back in a flash, pulling on protective gloves as I have to do. Danielle did not appear to have moved, and she was staring at me intently.

'This might sting a bit,' I said. 'But you're going to need it.'

I applied antiseptic cream and was relieved to see she'd already stopped bleeding. The wounds were not deep – they were more like scratches than cuts – and the white antiseptic cream stayed in place, sealing the skin.

'You know that boy, Harry?' she said, using a mumbling voice. 'He tried to feel me up.'

'He tried to feel you up?'

'Yes, and I let him. I quite fancy him. I told him that next time I stay at his house, I'll let him have sex with me. What would happen if I got pregnant?'

My head pounded; this was too much. I had to have strong words with her about this.

'Danielle, when you have sex with someone . . .' I started.

I suddenly thought about her past, and I stopped talking. I was going to say something like, 'it has to be special and you both have to be sure it's what you want.' But given what had happened to her, I knew I had to tread very carefully. The very last thing I wanted was to set her off on a dark train of thought at this point in time.

In the end I said something like, 'You are worth more than just letting a boy feel you up.'

'You are a smart, wonderful girl,' I added. 'You should wait until you meet someone special before you even think of doing anything at all. You are only thirteen.'

She nodded solemnly. 'Sorry. Shall we make the puddings now?'

'What?'

'The Yorkshire puddings, Angela. REMEMBER? Durgh! Is there anybody there?'

'Oh yes, come on. Let me put a big plaster on your arm first.'

Jonathan had gone out to pick up a few bits of shopping and to collect my mother on the way back. He'd been gone for less than twenty minutes and he couldn't believe what had happened in his absence.

'We'll have to report all of this first thing in the morning,' he said. 'I hate to say it, but I think we have to seriously consider whether this arrangement is tenable or not.'

I bit my lip. I was finding this the toughest placement we'd ever had, but I didn't want to give up.

'I don't want to fail. Danielle would be devastated if we had to tell her we couldn't let her stay any longer.'

'I know, Angela. I don't want to fail either, and I certainly don't want to add to Danielle's unhappiness. But maybe we don't have a choice. Maybe we are out of our depth.'

The words made me shudder, but I had to face facts. My doubts and fears about the placement were growing, and I had a horrible feeling creeping around my heart that wouldn't go away, no matter how hard I tried to stay positive and optimistic. It felt like *anything* could happen with Danielle, and that was a very disturbing thought.

16

'I. Want. To. Forget. Geddit, Angela?'

'I've spoken to Danielle's psychologist,' Susan said. 'I've gone through all the issues you've reported to date and asked for her opinion, in case there is anything she can tell us that might help.'

'Thank you, that's good to hear. We want to give Danielle all the help we can. What did the psychologist say?'

I'm not sure what I was expecting, but I was a little disappointed when Susan gave me her reply.

'She said that if Danielle makes any sort of disclosure or says anything you feel may be leading up to a disclosure, you are to repeat back to her what she has said. So, for example, if she says a boy tried to feel her up, you repeat, "A boy tried to feel you up?" with a questioning tone in your voice.'

'Right,' I said. 'That's what I do anyway. I was hoping for advice or some insight that might help me prevent Danielle from trying to harm herself. That's one of my biggest concerns at the moment, given what just happened with the roasting fork, and of course with her drinking the hand-wash. I'd like to understand as much as I can about her psychological make-up, so I can be as prepared and able as I possibly can be to look after her.'

Susan told me she understood my concerns but said she didn't have any further information from the psychologist. I asked if she could at least tell me if Danielle had been officially diagnosed with any kind of attachment disorder, or anything else? I asked this because by now I was starting to wonder if she perhaps had some other mental illness I was not aware of.

'If there has been an official diagnosis of any kind, it would be really useful to know about it,' I said.

'As I say, I don't have any further information, Angela. If the psychologist had anything she felt needed to be shared with Social Services, rest assured we would know about it and I would share it with you. But this is all I can tell you for the time being. Danielle is not a straightforward case, and her psychological assessments are ongoing. Of course, if you and Jonathan feel you'd like her to have another spell in respite care, that can certainly be arranged.'

I felt conflicted. I was not convinced Jonathan and I had the necessary skills to deal with Danielle, but then again, who did? The fact was, if she wasn't with us, she would just be with another set of foster carers – probably people she didn't know, who would be in the same boat as us in terms of their ability to deal with her. Therefore Danielle might possibly be at an even greater disadvantage, and that was the last thing any of us wanted. The upheaval of respite care just didn't seem worth it, although I didn't want to rule it out and it wasn't just my call in any case. If Social Services wanted to arrange it, they would have the final say.

'I'm open-minded about respite care,' I told Susan. 'I do recognise we need all the support we can get, but for now we'd like to carry on as we are. Please don't worry. I won't hesitate to ask for help if and when I think we, or Danielle, need another break.'

'That's sensible, Angela. I don't want you and Jonathan to burn out. Don't be afraid to ask for help. As I know you've heard before, it's not a sign of weakness or failure – quite the opposite.'

'We have to keep going and doing our best,' I said to Jonathan later.

'We do. Surely to goodness we can turn things around.'

'Yes. Surely we can?'

I said this with a question in my voice. It was wishful thinking, but was I being realistic?

That morning Danielle had offered to clean the bathroom, which I was delighted about. I praised her for being helpful and willing, and then I asked her if she wouldn't mind doing the vacuuming instead, as that was the next job that needed doing.

'You're a slave driver,' she said, her mood instantly shifting. 'You're the one who's supposed to be looking after me. You should be doing everything for me.'

'Danielle, you offered to help. I cleaned the bathroom yesterday and it doesn't need doing again this morning, so

I thought you could do the vacuuming instead, seeing as you've made such a kind offer to help.'

'It does need cleaning again. Scooter messed in there.'

'Did he?'

'Well, no, but he might have, because I let him go in there when I was cleaning my teeth.'

'OK. I'll check that. But if you are offering to help me, it would be great if you could vacuum the living room and the landing.'

'Oh, have it your way! Why don't you just get a whip or a big stick or a gigantic metal pole and hit me with it!'

Danielle said this in a confrontational way and she was clearly in one of her wind-up moods, but at the end of her outburst she suddenly had her faraway look on her face and appeared more uneasy than combative. In fact, she even seemed a little scared.

'Hit you?' I said, sensing she'd triggered a memory.

I wanted to add, 'I would never hit anyone, and nobody should ever hit you,' but I was being hyper-cautious about what I said, as I wanted Danielle to talk to me as freely as she possibly could, without being steered in any way at all.

'OK, I'll do the stupid vacuuming,' she said, gazing into space.

'Thanks,' I said.

'Don't mention it!'

Danielle went to fetch the vacuum cleaner from the cupboard in the utility room and lugged it up the stairs, clattering it on every step as she did so. I didn't tell her off;

it wasn't worth the scene I thought she might be trying to create.

I heard her switch the vacuum cleaner on and I heaved a heavy sigh. Danielle had such a knack of making even the simplest conversation or chore difficult. It was very draining, and her moods and the worrying things she said set me constantly on edge and made me very concerned about her. I felt stressed and nervous and protective towards her, all at the same time. It was like being outside when dark clouds gather, not knowing what will happen next. Will the clouds clear and let the sun shine through? Or will they explode into thunder and lightning, creating chaos and pouring cold water on everyone in their path?

'The vacuum cleaner's blown up!' Danielle suddenly yelled down the stairs.

She'd only been using it for a matter of minutes and I'd just heard it go off.

'Are you sure it's not the plug? Check it hasn't come loose in the socket. It happens sometimes.'

'No, it's blown up.'

I went upstairs to investigate, and sure enough the vacuum cleaner had packed up. There was a hot, rubbery smell, and I asked Danielle if she'd picked up anything that might have got stuck underneath and had maybe put a strain on the motor.

'Don't know what you mean,' she said, adding an unconvincing 'Oops' as she looked at the vacuum cleaner and shook her head mournfully.

I told her not to worry and said that Jonathan would have a look at it later, as he was handy with electrical things.

'No wonder Deirdre fancies him,' Danielle said, raising her eyebrows in a cheeky, goading way.

'I beg your pardon?'

'Deirdre, you know, my family-aid worker? She told me she fancies Jonathan.'

'Danielle, I think you've said quite enough.'

I did not for one moment think there was any truth in this and I did not want to discuss it further. I would have to tell Deirdre what Danielle had said, so everyone was in the picture, but I wasn't going to fall for Danielle's latest attempt at trouble-making, which I was sure it was. Deirdre was my friend as well as my colleague. I knew her well and it was completely unthinkable – outrageous, in fact – to even suggest she had said such a thing to Danielle.

'Anyway,' Danielle went on, sitting herself down on the carpet on the landing, crossing her legs. 'When I was little, my dad used to hit me, did you know that?'

'Your dad used to hit you?'

She cupped her chin in the palms of her hands and rested her elbows on her knees.

I sat down next to her, winding up the cable of the vacuum as I did so.

'He didn't like doing the cleaning, not like you! The house was dirty and messy. He hit me with lots of things. He hit me with the kettle once. It was lucky it had cold water in it, wasn't it? Or he might have burnt me too.'

'He might have,' I said softly, giving her a brief look in

the eye and then averting my gaze, so as to make her feel as comfortable as possible, to encourage her to carry on talking.

'It hurt when he hit me. It hurt so much I blacked out. Can you imagine that? I don't suppose you've ever blacked out from being hit, have you, Angela?'

She didn't wait for a reply. Instead she stared straight ahead and continued her monologue.

'Another time he hit me with a shovel, in the back yard. He said I'd come out of the shed when I should have stayed in it. But I didn't like the shed. It was cold and dark and I could hear a mouse scratching around. It freaked me out. I wanted to get out of there. Dad said the nosy old bag from next door might see me, and if he told me to stay in the shed, that was what I had to do, mouse or no mouse. "I don't care if there's a fuckin' grizzly bear in there, you stay put, geddit?" That's what he said. And when he said it he growled and he sounded scarier than a grizzly bear.'

Danielle glanced sideways at me, as if to check I was still listening. I tried to look calm and attentive, though inside I felt rage rising in my chest. I believed what she was telling me and I wanted to hug her and tell her she needed to tell me absolutely everything, and that her life would never be like that, ever again. Of course, I had no proof that any of what she said was actually true, but my gut reaction was very strong. This sounded like a genuine disclosure to me, and she was not finished yet.

'When he hit me with the shovel I had to go to A & E. He

228

told the nurses I climbed on the shed roof and fell off and hit my head on the concrete path. I didn't. I don't like heights, and I was only four anyway. He told me I had to lie to the nurses or he'd do something worse. I believed him. Once, did you know, a man took me to the top floor of a really high car park? He said he would throw me off the top. I would never climb on the shed roof. Dad hit me with the shovel, that's how my head got hit. I remember it. I remember what happened just before. He called me a "little bitch" and he swung the big shovel at me. I screamed. I saw the rusty metal right up close, like this, and then I can't remember anything else.' As she said the last sentence Danielle held her hands in front of her face to show how close the shovel got, and then she clapped her hands and said, 'BANG!'

I actually jumped. My nerves were jangling; I had a very vivid image of a four-year-old version of Danielle being hit by the big shovel.

'I was in hospital when I woke up. Afterwards Dad tried to make me feel better, or so he said. He gave me "grown-up medicine" to drink at home. It was vodka or gin, one of those clear ones. He put it in my beaker.'

She put her hand up to her mouth and pretended to drink.

'Glug glug glug. "Go on, Danni, drink it all up. It'll make you feel better." I didn't like the taste. I was sick lots of times, but I drank it anyway, because I didn't want to make him angry. I drank it before I went to work with my dad, because . . .' She looked up to the ceiling, a frozen expression on her face.

'Because?'

'I. Want. To. Forget. Geddit, Angela?'

Danielle turned to look at me. Her eyes were as black and hard as granite, with flinty flashes of light reflecting off them.

'You want to forget, Danielle. I heard what you said.'

'Good, because it wasn't just him, you know. He had a knife. He said he'd cut my throat if I told anyone, but I'm telling you. I've told her too. Maybe I'll have to kill you now I've told you. I can't kill her though. I wish I could.' She gave a hollow laugh, throwing her head back. Then she stared straight ahead again and went very still. 'And his friends had knives and other weapons.'

'Other weapons?'

'One had a screwdriver. He was so nasty, the worst of them all. He had tattoos and was scruffy and smelly. His beard was dirty and he had teeth missing. He held the screwdriver to my head and said he'd stab me with it if I told. He said all his friends had guns and they could kill me too. He said, "They wouldn't think twice, my girl. You 'ear me? You're nuffink."' Danielle put on a deep, gruff voice as she said this. '"You're nuffink but a little tramp. You're the lowest of the low, you 'ear me? Nobody would believe ya."'

I immediately realised I'd heard Danielle use similar words before, when she spoke about the homeless man she accused of raping her. *He's a tramp. He's the lowest of the low. Nobody would believe him anyway.* When she said that, Jonathan had questioned whether Danielle herself had been spoken to in that way, and it seemed his instincts were correct. This was devastating, and Danielle was still not done. Now she folded her arms in front of her and said bossily, 'I'll tell you another thing, Angela! This is not everything, oh no it isn't! I told you, you know nothing about me. You don't know me at all. You haven't got a clue. What do you know about what happened to me in the children's home?'

'The children's home? I know you were there in between your two foster placements. It was after leaving Granny and Pops, wasn't it?'

'Yes. But do you know what they did to me?'

'What they did to you?'

'The older kids. They were so mean. They burnt me with their cigarettes. They put them out on my arms and legs. Nobody believed me. The older kids said I did it myself, but I didn't. They had it in for me. They said I deserved it. They said I was a little slag.'

Danielle brushed her skirt down and got to her feet.

'Slag? How could I be a slag? I was ten years old. Fucking cheek. Now, where were we?' With that, she looked around in an exaggerated way, like a pantomime actress might when she wanted the audience to participate. 'What was it we were doing here, Angela? I can't remember? What happened here?'

I got to my feet too, and Danielle pointed to the vacuum cleaner.

'Ah, yes,' she said. 'I can't help you any more I'm afraid.'

'You can't help me?'

'That's right. I can't do any more because the vacuum cleaner has blown up, *remember*?' She rolled her eyes and swaggered towards her bedroom.

'Get Jonathan to fix it, will you?' she said as she reached her bedroom door. She looked for all the world like she might click her fingers and tell me to jump to it.

I let her go, and I took hold of the broken vacuum cleaner and carried it down to the landing on the floor below, standing it in the corner outside my bedroom. Then I went into my room and made a note of everything Danielle had told me.

When Jonathan heard all about it later, he cried.

'Did she cry?' he asked. 'When she was telling you all this?'

'No. Not a tear.'

We gave each other a knowing look. It seemed obvious Danielle had learned to hold her emotions in check when it came to dealing with the major traumas she had suffered.

'At least she's talking,' Jonathan conceded. 'It can only be a good thing, can't it?'

Despite all her previous lies and tall stories, Jonathan didn't doubt this was genuine disclosure either.

I nodded uncertainly.

'I hope you're right, Jonathan. I hope it's a good sign, that she's talking and letting go of things, but who knows?'

Normally when a child is going through a disclosing period it is considered progress. With Danielle, however, nothing was ever straightforward, and I wondered where this might lead to next.

Social Services took note of everything I passed on. I spoke to both Susan and Nelson, and two days later Susan came to visit us.

'Fancy a cup of tea?' I asked as soon as she arrived. I'd got to know Susan quite well by now. She looked like she'd been rushing, and she sank into a chair.

'Would love one, thanks, Angela. It's been one of those mornings, where I haven't got everything done that I wanted to, or at least that's what it's felt like.'

'Milk and sugar?'

'Milk, no sugar. The phone hasn't stopped ringing. There's been one problem after another. Ah, the joys of being a social worker!'

Fortunately, the two of us were able to have a talk before she saw Danielle. We carried on making general chit-chat while I made the tea, then Susan explained that she had spent several hours working on Danielle's disclosures.

'I've checked all the files, and none of the things Danielle has told you are down on any of our records. There's nothing about the physical violence she described at home, nothing about her being given alcohol by her father and no record of any threats to kill her from her dad or anybody else. Similarly, there is no report of her being taken to hospital.'

'Really? Surely a hospital visit would have been recorded. What do you think? Do you think Danielle has invented all of this?'

'It's very difficult to say, Angela, but we can't be certain she's telling the truth. However, what I can tell you is that the part of her story about her dad and his associates, about the violence and threats, is very similar to that of another girl she met at the children's home. Maybe it's a false memory or she's simply got muddled up? It can happen, especially when a child has been traumatised. Some children genuinely lose track of what is fact and what is fiction.'

'I see. She did seem to recall a lot of information about what happened to her. I guess perhaps too much detail for it to be credible, considering she's talking about her life at the age of five and under. I did believe her, although I guess I did wonder, too. It's very difficult, isn't it?'

'It is,' Susan said, sipping her tea and putting the mug down purposefully. 'Usually, as time passes, children start to have a rose-coloured view of what happened to them, wrongly remembering and believing that their childhood was good, or at least better than it actually was. In Danielle's case, she seems to be adding more distressing detail to what we already know and to what is on record. There is no doubt about the sexual abuse, of course. The men are in prison. But these other details, who knows?'

'And there's not even anything about her allegations of being burnt at the children's home?' I said, remembering how Danielle had talked in some detail about being burnt with cigarettes.

'Nothing. She was certainly unhappy there, that's clear. There are notes on file that state she was bullied, but not to the extent she is describing now. It was nasty name-calling and hair-pulling, according to the records. If she'd been burnt, that would need to be recorded and she'd have had medical treatment, but there's nothing on the file.'

We finished our tea and I took Susan upstairs to see Danielle, who was sitting in the living room watching one of her favourite DVDs. I'm sure she must have watched the same film at least six times in the last few months, and I can't imagine how many more times she had watched it before she moved in with us, but it never failed to enthral her.

'Can I finish watching this first?' she said when Susan and I appeared. As Danielle spoke she turned her head slightly towards us but kept her eyes glued to the screen.

'No, I'm afraid you can't,' I started, but Danielle immediately interrupted me and began asking Susan if she'd seen the film, and if she liked sci-fi and who her favourite *Star Wars* character was. Susan started to reply, but Danielle then interrupted her social worker and tried to talk to me again.

I walked across the room, paused the film and swapped a look with Susan.

'I'll leave you to it!' I said, smiling.

'Thanks a bunch!' Danielle replied.

I went downstairs, made myself another cup of tea and treated myself to a slice of cake. It was wedding cake, given to me by one of our regular customers in the shop, and I'd been looking forward to it. The young woman had got married the week before and we'd done all her flowers. While she was on honeymoon she got her mum to bring Jonathan and me a slice of her wedding cake, which I thought was really lovely. It was delicious too. I savoured every mouthful and also nibbled the marzipan and royal icing from Jonathan's slice, as he only likes the fruitcake.

'Ah, the joys of being a foster carer!' I thought as I tucked in.

After her chat with Danielle, Susan suggested we all might benefit from another respite weekend, sooner rather than later. I still had misgivings about the disruption this might cause to Danielle, but I trusted Susan's professional judgement. However, she then said the respite weekend could be arranged with the same family Danielle had stayed with last time.

'But what about the boy?' I asked. My immediate reaction was that I was alarmed and concerned this was an option, given what Danielle had said about the foster carer's son, and how she'd said she was considering having sex with him.

'We've spoken about that, Angela. Danielle has admitted she made the whole thing up. When I asked her why, she said it was because she'd quite like to have a boyfriend. It was all in her imagination and I have no concerns about her staying with the same family again. In an ideal world I'd put her in a single placement, I must admit, but only because she can be so demanding. However, the foster carer is extremely experienced and is willing to have Danielle again. It's the best option we have; you know how stretched we are at present.'

'Oh,' I said, thinking to myself, *At present? The fostering service is permanently stretched!*

'And I'm sure you'll be pleased to know that Danielle has admitted she made up the story about Deirdre taking a shine to Jonathan, too. She gave no explanation for that, but I think we can work it out.'

'Yes,' I said, 'Danielle seems to like upsetting the apple-cart, even if things are going well. It's such a shame.'

'Indeed – or *especially* when things are going well?' Susan commented. 'I've seen this behaviour in her before. She's not used to being happy, Angela. It's very sad, but I believe Danielle doesn't know how to deal with it when things are normal and safe and stable. You're doing an extremely good job with her. I take my hat off to you and Jonathan, I really do.'

I appreciated Susan's kind words, and the fact she'd taken the time to share her views and theories about Danielle's meddling behaviour, which I agreed with wholeheartedly. When I had a quiet moment to myself later, I found myself agonising about what Danielle had said. I had believed her 'disclosures'. I desperately didn't want to believe all those awful things had happened to her in addition to the sexual abuse she had suffered, but neither did I want to believe she was so troubled that she'd invented such stories, or falsely thought they were true.

'It's very hard to take all of this in, isn't it?' Jonathan said, appearing at the back door.

'Are you reading my mind again?' I joked.

'Yes, as a matter of fact I am. You need to stop searching

for answers you may never find and instead you need to give yourself a pat on the back, Angela. You've done brilliantly with Danielle. Well done.'

17

'I'll be out of your hair soon'

In the end it was agreed that Danielle would spend a weekend with Deirdre the next time she, and we, needed a break. It was Deirdre's idea, Social Services agreed and Jonathan and I felt it was a better plan than having Danielle staying in a foster home with two other teenagers, even if her stories about the thirteen-year-old boy there were fabricated.

I no longer felt a failure at the mention of Danielle having some respite care away from us. I acknowledged we all needed it, because her behaviour was getting more and more erratic. Ultimately, Jonathan and I agreed that railing against respite care would have been more of a failure than accepting it, for everybody's sake.

When we talked to Danielle about staying with Deirdre she seemed delighted.

'When will it be?'

'Let me see, in about ten days' time.'

'Great. It will be like a holiday, and it will be so good to stay in a *real* home.'

This seemed like a strange thing to say, because how was Deirdre's home any more 'real' than ours? Danielle elaborated, without me prompting her.

'The thing is, she's not a paid foster carer, is she? Deirdre's inviting me over as a friend. We'll have a good time. I won't get all that nagging I got at that respite carer's house.'

Again, I didn't argue; it wasn't worth it.

'I think you'll enjoy spending time at Deirdre's,' I said. 'It's always nice to have something to look forward to.'

'Yes, it is. And by the way, when are you taking me to see Granny and Pops again? What have you arranged, Angela?'

This was typical of the way Danielle was now speaking to me. The longer she was with us, the more she seemed to see me as some kind of servant when it suited her, but again I didn't feel it was a good idea to tackle her head-on about her attitude. I didn't want an argument. The truth was, I was constantly trying to minimise the chances of a blow-up. I could sense that one might be brewing, and I was treading carefully.

'We didn't arrange anything last time, did we? But we could give Granny and Pops a call and see what we can fix up. Shall we do that?'

'Yes please,' she said. 'Will you ring? I don't like using the phone.'

In my experience most thirteen-year-olds aren't keen on making phone calls. Even getting them to talk on the phone when the other person has made the call can be difficult; they'd typically much rather communicate with text messages – unless of course they are chatting non-stop to their 'best' friend. Danielle's remark suddenly reminded me about her claims she had called Glennis and Mike at the start of her placement. I still had no idea whether or not Danielle had really phoned them and it didn't matter any more. She hadn't mentioned them for a long while, and I now thought it was unlikely she had ever contacted them. I knew Danielle so much better than I had a few months earlier. I knew she was very good at spinning tales, and the more I got to know her, the more I treated what she said with a healthy dose of scepticism.

I phoned Iris and, happily, she invited Danielle over the following morning.

'Wicked!' Danielle said.

After that Danielle seemed to be in a very good mood for the rest of the day. Mum came over and they played dominoes and Cluedo and watched an old black-and-white movie.

'Can I get you anything, Thelma?' Danielle checked before they settled in front of the TV.

'No thank you, dear.'

'OK, well, just let me know.'

If you didn't know better, you'd have thought Danielle was the model of a perfect child.

Later, Danielle cleaned out Scooter's cage in the utility room. She played with him for ages, chattering away to him like a small child might, seemingly completely oblivious to her surroundings.

'What an imagination she has!' Mum said as she sipped

a cup of coffee in the kitchen. 'Have you heard the conversations she's having, Angela? How delightful.'

I wasn't tuned in to what Danielle was saying to Scooter as I was busy preparing dinner while she played with him on the floor in between the kitchen and utility room. Now I made a point of listening as I topped and tailed some runner beans Mum had brought from her garden. Danielle was asking lots of random questions, such as, 'What do you dream about?' and 'What would *you* buy if you found £100?' Then she pretended to listen to what Scooter said, holding him up to her ear. 'No way! I have the same dream. Do you wish you could change it? I do. If I found £100 I'd buy a shield and a coat of armour. No, I wouldn't waste it on birthday cake. No way!'

And so it went on.

'Isn't it lovely?' Mum said. 'It's quite endearing to witness such innocence in a thirteen-year-old, isn't it?'

I smiled and nodded. Mum knew nothing about Danielle's past or about the troubles she had, and that was the way it should be.

'It's time for bed,' I said to Danielle at the end of the evening. 'You've got a busy day tomorrow.'

'OK,' she said cheerfully, getting to her feet. 'Night night, Thelma. Thanks for the games. It was good to see you!'

'You too. Goodnight, darling. Sleep well!'

As Danielle crossed the room I spotted the back of her trousers was wet and glanced at the chair she'd been sitting on – the one I'd covered in plastic. Danielle had clearly had an accident and so I followed her to the door, walking closely behind her to prevent Mum from noticing.

'Sweetheart, you'll need to have a shower before bed,' I said softly.

'OK,' she said. 'But can I use your bathroom because my showerhead is broken again.'

'Is it? How did that happen?'

'Dunno.'

'OK. Go and fetch your towel first, so you have it ready.'

Danielle agreed and I told her I'd come up and say goodnight soon.

'OK!' she said brightly. 'I'll just have a quick shower.'

I discreetly cleaned the chair and Jonathan said he'd take Mum home. He had to get some petrol while he was out, and he asked if we needed anything from the garage.

'No, we're fine, thanks. Maybe just get a pint of milk as I used a lot in the egg custard and we're running a bit low.'

'OK, no problem.'

I said goodbye to Mum, emptied the dishwasher and gave the kitchen floor a quick sweep before I went up to say goodnight to Danielle. She wasn't in her room, so I went down to the floor below to see if she was still in my bathroom. I could hear the shower was still running, even though Danielle had said she was only having a quick shower.

'Danielle,' I called, knocking on the door. 'Are you all right?'

She didn't reply. I knocked again, this time a bit louder.

'Danielle. You've been rather a long time in there. Can you hear me?'

Again there was no reply and so I tried once more.

'Danielle, can you get out of the shower now? Are you all right?'

I had an unsettling feeling in my stomach and I found myself wishing Jonathan was in the house and I was not alone with Danielle.

'Danielle, if you don't answer me I'm going to have to come in and check you are all right.'

Still she didn't reply.

'OK, I'm going to come in, Danielle. I'm going to open the door from this side. Can you hear me?'

We had one of those bathroom locks you could open from the outside by putting a coin in the slot in the handle and turning it. This had caused problems in the past, with one child in particular making trouble by deliberately breaking into the bathroom when another child was using it. I wished then that it wasn't so easy to unlock the doors, but now I was very glad we had this type of lock. I fetched a coin from my bedside table and opened the bathroom door after knocking really loudly one last time, calling to Danielle to tell her what I was doing.

'Danielle?' I said as I opened the door. I didn't want to barge in in case she wasn't covered up, so I peered from the doorway. The room was filled with so much steam it took a moment to spot her. When the steam cleared a little I saw Danielle sitting on the toilet, wearing soaking wet clothes.

'Are you all right, sweetheart?'

'No, but what do you care?'

'I do care. What happened?'

'She made me, stupid cow!'

'Who?'

'That woman, whatever her name is. Stupid cow!'

'Who?'

'Oh, it doesn't matter, does it? I'll be out of your hair soon.'

With that Danielle suddenly lunged forward and grabbed a bottle of shampoo. Before I had a chance to realise what she was up to she began trying to squirt it in her mouth.

'Stop it!' I said, taking firmly hold of the bottle and just about managing to stop her. 'You can't put that in your mouth.'

'I hate you! You spoil everything. Your mum is nicer than you! Everyone is nicer than you!'

'Danielle, please calm down. I'm here to help you.'

'How can you help me? Nobody can help me.'

She stared out of the window, or should I say at the steamed-up glass of the window.

'Danielle, you are going to get cold in those wet clothes. Please can you get yourself out of them, dry yourself off and put on your pyjamas.'

'Of course I can, do you think I'm some kind of baby?'

'No, I don't.'

'Then I'll do it!'

'Right. Here's your towel. Dry yourself off here and then go to your room and put on your pyjamas, please.'

'OK, OK! Nag, nag, nag. You should be called Nag-ela, not Ang-ela. I think you've got the letters muddled up!'

I scooped up the shampoo and conditioner, the shower gel and my tube of toothpaste, as I didn't want Danielle to have a go at putting anything else in her mouth.

'I'll come up and see you very shortly. Please be as quick as you can.'

As I left the bathroom I noticed my toothbrush was on the side of the washbasin – a big mistake. I make a point of removing my toothbrush if a child is using my bathroom, but I'd forgotten on this occasion. I didn't trust what Danielle might have done with it, because in the past I've had children tell me they've stuck my toothbrush down the toilet or cleaned their toenails with it. I never knew if they were telling the truth or just taunting me, but of course it wasn't worth taking any chances. With Danielle, I really could not be sure what she might have done in that room. Her behaviour was unpredictable and untrustworthy in the extreme. I threw the toothbrush in the bin, and willed Jonathan to get home quickly.

When I finally got Danielle into bed I felt shattered, but that was not the end of the drama. Later, just as I was falling asleep, I heard Danielle padding around upstairs. It sounded like she was opening and closing doors and deliberately making a noise. I got straight out of bed and went to investigate.

'Shall I come with you?' Jonathan asked.

We looked at each other in alarm. Had it got so bad that

I needed protection to go and check on Danielle in her bedroom?

'No, I can deal with this, thanks.'

It seemed ridiculous that a thirteen-year-old girl could instil fear in either of us, and I was determined not to go down that road. When I got upstairs I found Danielle sitting on the floor of her bathroom. Both taps and the shower were running, and there was water everywhere. The door to the shower cubicle was open and as the showerhead was broken, water was squirting in all directions. Danielle had the window wide open too, and there was a cigarette stubbed out on the windowsill.

'Right, let's sort this out,' I said, taking a deep breath.

I switched off the taps and the shower and, before I dealt with the water on the floor and splattered up the walls, I asked Danielle for her cigarette lighter.

'Haven't got it,' she said. She was hugging her knees, rocking back and forth and staring into space.

'I can see you've had a cigarette up here. You've left the butt on the windowsill. Please give me the lighter. You know the rules. If you are going to smoke, you do it out of the house, and I look after your lighter in the house.'

'Can't give it to you.'

'Why?'

'I threw it out the window. What are you going to do about that, An-ge-la?'

I wasn't entirely sure. I'd never had to deal with so many random problems all at once, and I'd never been so unsure about whether a child was telling the truth or not. Danielle was capricious, unreliable and impetuous: an incredibly demanding combination.

I quickly took stock and made a decision. It was late, I didn't think Danielle was going to smoke again this evening – in fact she'd probably only smoked that one cigarette so I would find it – and I had to do everything in my power to keep her calm and get her to bed, and asleep, without further incident.

'You have two choices, Danielle,' I said. 'You can go and find the lighter now and give it to me, and I'll come with you to search the garden, or you can go to bed quietly and without a fuss, and we'll talk about this in the morning, before you go to Granny and Pop's.'

'Can I still go?'

'Yes.'

'Right. I'll go to bed. I'm tired. It's far too late. How could you even think about going into the garden now? Are you crazy?'

I bit my tongue as I scanned the bathroom. By rights I knew I should get Danielle to help me clean this mess up, but I just wanted her in her bed and out of my way. The sooner she was fast asleep and this day ended, the better.

I gave the bathroom a wipe down and, after checking Danielle's light was off and all was quiet, I went back to bed myself.

'Everything OK?' Jonathan asked.

When I described what had happened he sat up and put the light on, which was very unusual for my husband. Normally Jonathan soothes away my fears, encourages me to get some sleep and tells me everything will look better in the morning.

'This is a nightmare,' he said. 'Do you think she still has the lighter in her room?'

'No, I don't. I believe she threw it out of the window. Besides, I'm not worried about her starting a fire or trying to burn something. I think she smoked that cigarette as an act of defiance, to wind me up.'

'Yes, that fits. That definitely fits.'

I reminded Jonathan that Danielle was not a fire-starter, as I could tell this was playing on his mind again.

'I know. I'm just not at ease though.'

'Me neither, but I guess if we let her see that, she's won. She wants to get our backs up – and mine especially. We should try to get some sleep.'

'Yes, we should. I'm shattered, to tell the truth.'

'Me too.'

'Let's hope she'll be in a better mood when she sees Iris and Kenneth tomorrow.'

'She'll probably be sweetness and light, just like she is with Mum!'

As I spoke I heard a noise outside our bedroom door. I whispered to Jonathan and got out of bed as quietly as I could, creeping across the carpet and slowly opening the door. As I suspected, Danielle was standing there, right outside our bedroom door.

'Danielle! What are you doing? I thought you were in bed.'

'I lost an earring,' she said. 'I thought it might be on the carpet here.'

She'd jumped back when I opened the door. It seemed obvious she'd been trying to listen in on our conversation.

'We'll look in the morning. Which one is it?'

'The triangle one.'

'You're wearing your triangle earrings, Danielle. Both of them.'

'Oops. Sor-ree. I'll go to bed now. Don't worry; I shan't be winding you up any more tonight, especially you, Angela. I don't want to get your back up!'

Jonathan and I didn't sleep until the house had been in absolute silence for quite some time.

18

'I AM LOOKING FOR SOMETHING TO STAB YOU WITH!'

Jonathan was up at the crack of dawn, and he found Danielle's cigarette lighter lying in the middle of the back lawn.

'Thank God for that,' he said. 'And thank God she has a busy day ahead.' As well as visiting Iris and Kenneth, Danielle was going out with Deirdre in the afternoon.

'I'll ring Nelson when she's out, fill him in. I think I'll call Iris too, just to give her the heads-up.'

'Good idea.'

Danielle appeared at the kitchen door.

'Good morning!' she said sunnily. 'I've got wet sheets, shall I put them straight in the washing machine?'

'Yes please. I'll get the washing done while you are out at Granny and Pop's. Have you remembered you are going to see them this morning?'

'Yes. Thank you for letting me go. Sorry about last night. I don't know why I did all that.'

I looked at Jonathan and gave him the nod. We'd talked

about how to handle this, and we'd decided to try to encourage more good behaviour and reduce the drama in the
house by making a deal with Danielle.

'I've been talking to Angela,' Jonathan said. 'And we
think you need a very good incentive, to help you improve
your behaviour. None of us want a repeat of what happened
last night. It was such a shame things went wrong the way
they did after you'd had such a pleasant time with Thelma.'

'I know, but I can't help it, that's the thing. I don't want
to be bad!'

This was something Jonathan and I had discussed. Was
it actually worth dangling a carrot in front of Danielle to try
to encourage good behaviour, if she truly could not control
herself? We came to the conclusion it *was* worth it, because
where else could we go? Punishing her was out of the question. We didn't even use the word punishment, as I've said
before. Putting consequences in place didn't seem to make
much of a difference either, as she reverted to bad behaviour regardless.

'You're not bad,' I said, 'but sometimes your behaviour
is. Jonathan and I have decided we'll take you on a day trip
to London, provided you can do three things.'

'London? What for? I've never been to London.'

'We thought it would be nice to visit the Crown Jewels,
as a reward for good behaviour.'

'OK,' she said suspiciously. 'What do I have to do? Is it
hard?'

It was Jonathan's turn to talk. We'd decided that if he lay
down the rules of the challenge, Danielle might respond

more positively than if this came from me. 'It's not very hard, not for a smart girl like you,' he said. 'What we want is for you to be polite, helpful, and to stop and think before you act.'

'That's easy!'

'It should be, because we know you can do it. We've seen you be polite and helpful, and we know you can behave well. You do it with Thelma all the time. We're very proud of you when you behave so beautifully with Thelma. What we want is for you to be like that with us. We want you to stop yourself if an idea comes into your head that might not be a good one.'

'But it's not always my fault . . . I can't help it.'

'I think you can do better if you really try. That's true of all of us. So, next time you think you might make a mess or maybe smoke in the house or say something rude, we want you to stop yourself and think about the consequences. We want you to think about how you will feel after you have mis-behaved, how Angela and I will feel and what will happen next – or should I say, what will not happen. You won't be able to go on the day trip to London if you haven't been behaving well enough, so you need to show us what you can do.'

Danielle thought for a moment and smiled.

'It's a deal,' she said. 'Let's shake on it!'

She shook Jonathan's hand first, then mine. She ate her breakfast without incident and got ready on time, with not a single problem.

'So far so good,' I said to Jonathan.

'Don't get too carried away,' he joked. 'We're less than an hour in!'

I gave Iris a potted summary of recent events over the phone, while Jonathan drove Danielle to their bungalow.

'I don't know what it is with bathrooms,' Iris lamented. 'Soaking the floor, as well as anything left lying around the bathroom, was one of her habits when she was with us. I had to get rid of the cloth bathmats in the end and get a wooden one as I was forever trying to dry them out. As for the smoking business, Kenneth has a theory about that. Did you know she was bullied at the children's home?'

'Yes, we did.'

'Well, that was when she started to smoke, when she was ten. Kenneth reckons it was her way of trying to be more of an equal to the older kids, to try to stop them bullying her.'

Iris also went on to explain that the other kids at the home continually complained that Danielle was being better treated than they were. It seemed that Danielle was so unpopular with the other kids that the staff would take her out on trips to the cinema or ice skating or bowling, just to give everyone else a peaceful day. The other kids felt Danielle was getting rewarded for her bad behaviour, which seemed perfectly understandable. They said she was 'pampered' and called her a 'big baby'.

'It sounds like a feasible theory, about why she started smoking,' I replied. 'And maybe now it still fits. Maybe she's smoking when she wants to appear grown up or to be in control? It's a way of asserting herself perhaps, and making a point that she's not a small child any more?' As I said that I thought to myself, *No wonder she can't wait to leave her childhood behind and be a grown-up*, but I didn't say it out loud.

'That holds water,' Iris said. 'She's certainly a tough nut to crack though, isn't she, Angela?'

I could picture Iris giving a kind and understanding smile as she said this, and it made me smile too. Iris had a way of lightening the tone of the conversation even when the subject matter was incredibly heavy.

'She is indeed. I hope she's good for you today, Iris, and thanks for having her.'

'No problem. Any time. Now you look after yourself, and remember this; it's a quote someone printed out for me years ago, when Kenneth and I first started fostering.'

I listened as Iris read the quote, which she explained she still had pinned on her kitchen notice board. '*Will it be easy? Nope. Worth it? Absolutely.*'

I relayed this to Jonathan when he returned. 'How true,' he commented.

'Well, I hope so,' I said.

'Have confidence, Angela. It will be worth it, in the end.'

Jonathan picked Danielle up after lunch, so she'd be home in time to be collected by Deirdre, who was taking her out that afternoon. Iris and Kenneth said she'd been a pleasure to have. They'd done some baking and looked at old photographs from when Danielle lived with them, and she was in a really good mood when Jonathan collected her.

In the car on the way home Danielle asked Jonathan if we could be her 'forever family' now.

'We'd love you to stay for longer, but I can't say for definite what is going to happen. Social Services are still trying to get you into a school, and as you know there aren't many places available. Even though there is nothing right now, it could change and it could be that they find you a school you'd have to live closer too.'

'Do you think that will happen? It's not looking likely after all this time, is it? Is that what you want?'

'I want what's best for you, Danielle. We'll all have to talk about that if and when a place comes up. All we know for sure is that for the next few months you're staying with us.'

'Is that definite?'

'It's what we all agreed after the last big placement meeting, isn't it?'

'Yes, but what if I can't behave?'

'What if you *can* behave? I know you can. You've just behaved really well with Iris and Kenneth.'

'Yes, but they're old and I wouldn't want to upset them.'

'But surely you wouldn't want to upset anyone? Why would you want to upset anyone?'

'Yes, but . . . Forget it. You're just like Angela. You don't get it. It's not me. It's not my choice. You'd never understand even if you lived to be a hundred years old!'

'I'd like to understand.'

'Well, so would I, thank you very much! Now how long have I got to get ready before Deirdre arrives? I don't even want to go out with her today. It's all rush, rush, rush and nag, nag, nag. Put your foot down, will you, Jonathan? I'd at least like five minutes to myself at some point today, if that's not too much to ask!'

Jonathan put a Take That CD on in the car and stopped talking. He knew when to call it quits, and thankfully Danielle spent the rest of the short journey back to our house gazing out of the window.

I was in the shop when they got back and Danielle popped in to see me. I was preparing a bouquet and Danielle watched as I curled the pink ribbon into ringlets after tying it around the flowers.

'You're so good at that, can you train me how to do it?'

'Yes, when we've got more time. I'd love to show you.'

I'd tried to encourage Danielle to help a little around the shop, as I normally do with all the teenagers who stay with us. If they're willing and interested we sometimes give them a bit of holiday or weekend work, to help teach them how to deal with the public and to give them the chance of earning some extra cash. Danielle had point-blank refused to have anything to do with the shop until now, and in fact she'd accused me of trying to exploit her when I suggested she could help out.

I was very pleased she'd changed her attitude, and I told her I'd make sure I fixed up a bit of 'training' as soon as possible.

'Cool, thanks, Angela. Maybe I'll be a florist when I grow up.'

'If you'd like to learn, I'll teach you how to do a few more things, other than just tying bouquets,' I said. 'Would you like that?'

'Yes. Maybe I could stay here forever, and take over the shop when you and Jonathan are too old to run it yourselves. What do you say?'

I smiled at her cheekiness; it was lovely to be around her when she was in this kind of playful mood.

A customer came in the door.

'Right, Danielle, you had better get ready for your outing with Deirdre. Excuse me while I serve this customer. Hope you have a good time.'

'Thanks,' she said, suddenly giving me one of her strange smiles.

The customer asked me about a display in the front window, and I left the counter to go and serve her. Danielle loitered for a moment before saying goodbye.

'Look forward to seeing you later, Angela. Have a good afternoon!'

I heard the back door of the shop clatter shut as Danielle made her way through to the house. Was she up to something or was I just being paranoid? *You're being paranoid, Angela. She's in a lovely mood. Enjoy it while it lasts!*

When Deirdre collected Danielle she called in to the shop to tell me they were going to play badminton at the local sports centre and maybe have a walk around the lake in the park, if the weather stayed fine.

'Sounds good,' I said. 'I'm not a hundred per cent sure what mood she's in. I hope it goes well.'

'I'm sure it will,' Deirdre said, adding with a conspiratorial but kindly smile, 'Do we ever know what mood she's in? See you later, Angela!'

Hatty also called in to the shop an hour or so afterwards as she was passing and popped in on the off-chance we could have a catch-up. I hadn't seen her for a few weeks so there was quite a lot to tell her.

'Shall I come with you on the trip to London, if you make it?' she offered, after hearing all about our latest ups and downs.

'I think that's a terrific idea,' I said. 'Danielle would love it. It will add to the incentive if I tell her you'd like to come, I'm sure. And it will hopefully help her stay on good behaviour, once we're there.'

'Great. Keep me posted. I'm looking forward to it already. Please tell her that, won't you?'

'Yes. I'm sure Jonathan and I will enjoy it more too, with you there. It will be great to have you with us. I sometimes think Danielle needs more than two carers!'

Hatty nodded. 'There's a lot of truth in that,' she said.

I was feeling positive after seeing Hatty, but then Jonathan came into the shop shortly after Danielle had returned with Deirdre, and in an instant everything suddenly changed.

'Whatever's the matter?'

'It's Danielle. She's in a terrible state. She's stormed upstairs and I'm afraid she's gearing up for another blow-up.'

'What's happened? Did she say anything?'

'She shouted and swore and complained as she came in the house, but she isn't making much sense. She looks like a mad woman. Her eyes are scary, and if looks could kill . . .'

'Oh my goodness. Is Deirdre still here?'

'Yes, she's in the kitchen. She said she'll stay a while. She can't understand what's gone wrong. They had a good game of badminton and went to the park and the lake afterwards, and the cafe for a drink and a snack, but apparently Danielle's mood switched in the car on the way home, completely out of the blue.'

'What on earth could have brought this on?'

'Who knows? It's awful, Angela. Danielle is absolutely blazing with anger. She threw her badminton kit all over the hallway before she stormed upstairs. I could see she'd wet herself too, and she shouted down the stairs that she wants to die.'

'Oh God. Will you take over here and I'll go and talk to Deirdre?'

'No, you stay here. I'd like to deal with this, at least for now. I've put the kettle on and Deirdre's in the kitchen. I'll get back to her, if you're OK to shut up on your own?'

'Yes,' I said, glancing at the clock. Fortunately it was early closing day and I told Jonathan I'd shut the shop up as quickly as possible and join him and Deirdre in the kitchen.

My heart was pounding as I hauled in the displays from outside, pulled down the shutters and cashed up the till at break-neck speed. I darted through to the house, wondering what I'd find. To my surprise the place was in total silence, and Jonathan was sitting at the bottom of the stairs.

'I've been up to Danielle's room and she's told me to go away and she never wants to see me again. I'm sitting here listening, in case I'm needed. Deirdre is up there now.'

'Was Danielle OK with her?'

'Yes. She seemed much more receptive to Deirdre than to me.'

'Right. Do you think we should both go up together, see if Deirdre is OK?'

'Yes, let's do that.'

Jonathan and I went upstairs and tapped on Danielle's door.

'Fuck off, both of you,' she said. 'I don't need you two here.'

Deirdre called for us to come in. Jonathan opened the door and as he did so Danielle immediately jumped up, grabbed a tube of cream from her dressing table and squirted it in her mouth. Jonathan made a grab for the tube and managed to take it off her, but not before Danielle had managed to swallow some of its contents. It was a tube of antiseptic cream and a brand I didn't recognise and had never bought. Where had she got that?

'Urgh! Urgh!' Danielle was gagging in an exaggerated way, and she dropped to her knees as she retched. Nothing came up and she sat frozen-faced, staring at the wall and with white cream smeared around her mouth. She wouldn't let Deirdre, Jonathan or me near her and told us all to stay away from her.

'I'm calling the emergency doctor,' Jonathan said. 'I'll be as quick as I can.'

While Jonathan went to make the call, Deirdre and I both sat silently on the edge of Danielle's bed, keeping a close eye on her. The two of us watched as she slowly rose to her feet. She looked unsteady and her eyes were glazed.

'Danielle, have you taken anything else?' Deirdre asked gently.

She didn't reply but instead began to walk erratically around her room, opening and closing drawers and cupboards, as I'd seen her do in the kitchen on several occasions. The difference this time was that Danielle looked so wound up she seemed quite deranged; this was not the childish Danielle in action, this was the aggressive, foul-tempered and extremely unpredictable Danielle at work.

'What are you looking for?' I asked. 'Can I help you, Danielle? Why don't you sit down and let us help?'

Danielle had her back to Deirdre and me and she was breathing very slowly and deeply and was pointedly ignoring us. The atmosphere was incredibly hostile, and Danielle's behaviour was starting to frighten me. Deirdre looked very uneasy too. I wished Jonathan would come back, but I knew it could take a while to get through to the emergency doctor, and then he would have to read out all the ingredients of the antiseptic cream so the doctor could tell us whether or not we needed to take Danielle to hospital.

'WHAT AM I LOOKING FOR? I AM LOOKING FOR SOMETHING TO STAB YOU WITH!' Danielle suddenly shouted, turning round to face me.

Deirdre was on her feet in an instant.

'Come on, Danielle, let's go out into the garden and get

some fresh air. Angela, you stay there. Now come on, Danielle, I'd like you to take a big, deep breath and come with me . . .'

Thankfully, Danielle allowed Deirdre to steer her out of the room, down the stairs and out to the back garden. I let out a huge sigh of relief as I heard them walk away. What had this placement come to and why was it going so terribly wrong? I wanted Danielle to see how much I cared for her, but it was as if the more I tried, the more she kicked out at me. Now she had threatened to physically attack me. It was unbelievable, and I felt swamped with sadness and despair.

19

'What is wrong with Danielle?'

Jonathan was horrified when he found out what Danielle had said to me. He gave me a big hug and said we'd better go down to the living room immediately, so we could phone Social Services and catch Nelson while the office was still open.

Before we left Danielle's bedroom, Jonathan scanned the room for any harmful objects or substances. He had already removed the antiseptic cream, and now he took a pencil sharpener off Danielle's desk and a bottle of sun cream from her dressing table.

He trod on something as we made our way out of the room.

'What are these doing here?' he asked, alarmed.

A pair of my floristry scissors was on the floor, hidden by some sheets of scrap paper.

'Oh God, I was showing her how to do ribbons earlier,' I said, feeling shocked. 'I thought she acted a bit strangely as she left the shop. I shut up in such a rush I didn't realise they were missing.'

'OK,' Jonathan said firmly, recognising the fear in my voice. 'We mustn't jump to conclusions. Even though Danielle had the scissors in her room and said what she did, it doesn't mean she would actually carry out her threat. It's just an expression of anger, I'm sure.'

'I hope you're right, but this is a terrible situation, isn't it?'

'It is. Come on, we need to call Nelson.'

Thankfully, the emergency doctor had told Jonathan that Danielle didn't need to go to hospital, as the amount of cream she might have swallowed would not be enough to cause her any harm. At least that was one less problem we had to deal with. We got hold of Nelson straight away and told him everything. He checked that all was calm and everybody was safe before telling us he would refer up to a senior manager about what to do next.

As soon as we finished the call we heard Deirdre bring Danielle in from the garden and into the kitchen, and so Jonathan and I went down to see them. We found Danielle sitting silently at the table, looking like she was smouldering with anger. Her eyes were full of fury and she was biting her nails aggressively and huffing and puffing. Deirdre was sitting quietly beside her.

I told Deirdre I'd called Nelson, but as soon as I mentioned his name Danielle flew into a rage.

'You're a liar! You tell Nelson lies all the time. You hate

me; I know you do, Angela. Why did you take me in if you were going to spread lies behind my back?'

I was lost for words and looked to Deirdre for support. She took me to one side and said she had an idea about what we could do next.

'It's something that has worked well before. Before I go on, I take it you and Jonathan are both free now?'

'Yes, it was early closing today. The shop's shut.'

I had been planning to go to an evening exercise class I had recently taken up, but I had already written it off in my mind. I wasn't in the mood at all, and I needed to prioritise Danielle. This was a serious situation, and I wanted the best possible outcome, for all of us. We all needed to pull together and do whatever it took to help Danielle get over this and move on.

Deirdre briefly explained her idea to me. I agreed with her suggestion. We ran it past Jonathan, and then Deirdre walked back across the kitchen to speak to Danielle.

'Danielle, how are you feeling?'

'How do you THINK I'm feeling, Deirdre?' Danielle blurted out angrily. 'I'm wound up, Deirdre. That's how I'm feeling. And you would feel the same if you were in my shoes, let me tell you!'

'I can see that you're wound up, and I have an idea. Why don't we drive out into the countryside? I think it would be good to get out of the house, and you could let off some steam, in the open air.'

'I've just had fresh air in the garden. What's the point? What good will that do?'

'Well, in the countryside you can run around, scream and shout as loudly as you want, and just let out all your anger, out there in the open.'

Danielle shrugged but seemed to soften a little.

'I'm not a crazy person, you know.'

'I'm not suggesting you are.'

Deirdre lowered her voice and, in a confidential tone, added, 'I've done this myself on the odd occasion, to tell you the truth. Once, when I'd had a very hard and irritating day at work, I went out on my own and found a quiet spot in the woods and screamed at the trees. I felt so much better afterwards.'

'You did? Are you serious?'

'I'm very serious. It helped me no end. I think maybe it could help you too.'

'I don't know.'

'What have you got to lose? If it doesn't help, it doesn't help. But I think it could.'

'Suppose,' Danielle muttered. 'I bet Angela's asked you to get me out of the house, get rid of me. Is that it?'

'No, this is my idea. And actually I'm going to ask Angela and Jonathan to come along with us.'

'Why?'

'I think it's a good idea.'

'Right. So, if I do this, does it mean I won't get thrown out or locked up?'

'Danielle, the whole point of me making this suggestion is to help you. Angela, Jonathan and I all want to help you. We are not looking for ways to make your life more difficult.

We don't want you thrown out or locked up. We all want to *improve* your life.'

'Why?'

'Because we care.'

'I bet Angela doesn't care any more, now she knows I want to stab her, if she ever did care in the first place. She only looks after me for the money, you know. She hates me really. She's been looking for ways to get rid of me. I know all about it. She's jealous that I get on better with Jonathan than I do with her, did you know that? That's the truth. Angela doesn't care about me ONE BIT.'

Danielle was speaking about me as if I was in another room, even though I was standing quietly on the other side of the kitchen.

'I know for a fact that none of these things are true,' Deirdre soothed. 'Angela cares very deeply about you.'

Deirdre gestured for me to step closer, and gave me a nod. I took my cue, while Danielle glared at me.

'Sweetheart, I care about you very much. I want to help you. I want you to be happy. As I've told you before, I want to help you carve out a good future for yourself, the future you deserve. You're a lovely girl and I understand you have had difficulties in your life. I don't judge you or blame you for anything that has happened to you in the past that might make you behave badly now. Honestly, I don't have to be a foster carer. I work as a foster carer because I want to look after children like you. I choose to do it.'

I paused. Danielle looked thoughtful, and I dared to hope I'd got through to her.

'Shall we all go for that drive?' I asked, giving her a smile. 'I think it's a good idea, and so does Jonathan.'

'Oh for God's sake. I don't suppose I have much choice!'

Jonathan and I had never used Deirdre's proposed method of calming a child down before, although we'd heard of similar scenarios through our training. We trusted in Deirdre completely, and we were very glad of her assistance.

Just before leaving I took a phone call from Nelson.

'Positive news. We've got an emergency place in a children's home. The bosses think that is the best option for Danielle, for the time being. She can't stay with you after what has happened.'

'OK,' I stuttered, feeling shocked and deflated at the speed of developments.

'So it's a temporary measure, I take it? How long do you think she will be there? And when will she move in?'

'It's going to be tomorrow at the earliest, and hopefully it will be a short-term measure, but we're not sure.'

Nelson then explained that Danielle would have a medical assessment while she was at the children's home, and that he needed to fix up a night of respite care for her, this evening. His seniors at Social Services had decided this was the safest course of action, given Danielle's threat to me.

'We'd like her to stay at Deirdre's house tonight if that is possible. Is Deirdre still with you?'

'Yes, we were just leaving to take Danielle into the countryside to try and let off some steam, so to speak.' I explained the plan to Nelson and he approved, but only because all three adults were accompanying Danielle.

'OK. Safety is the priority right now, for everybody. Can I have a word with Deirdre?' he asked.

I put Deirdre on the phone and she immediately agreed to have Danielle overnight.

'Yes, I agree and I think it's the safest option,' Deirdre said, nodding as she spoke to Nelson. 'And I'll take Danielle to the children's home in the morning. I look forward to hearing more details. Yes, I'll have another adult with me. No problem.'

Deirdre also confirmed to Nelson that there was no need to take Danielle to A & E, explaining that the very small amount of antiseptic cream she may have imbibed was not toxic.

I felt absolutely terrible as I began to take in the enormity of what was happening. Danielle was moving out, tonight. This seemed like a dreadful failure on mine and Jonathan's part, but at the same time I had to agree that keeping Danielle with us was not safe in her volatile state, at least not in the short term. I wondered if perhaps she'd have been OK just with Jonathan, but it was irrelevant really: I didn't trust how she would behave with me and so that was the end of it. I knew I would not be able to sleep if Danielle was still in the house. Any trust I had in her had been called into question and I knew that if she stayed with us I'd be wondering what she might do next, and worrying.

It was terrible to work through these thoughts. I could see that my relationship with Danielle was very broken right now, and although it was the very last thing I wanted to accept, it was starting to dawn on me that her placement was quite possibly damaged beyond repair. Maybe she would never return to us? I shuddered; it was a very alarming possibility.

We all set off in the car. Deirdre sat in the back with Danielle while Jonathan drove and I sat in the passenger seat. As we headed out into the countryside Deirdre explained to Danielle what would happen, that evening and the next day. Deirdre told Danielle she could collect a bag of belongings from our house after our little trip out, and then she would be going to stay the night in her home. The next day Danielle would move straight from Deirdre's house into the children's home.

'For how long?'

'That, we don't know, I'm afraid,' Deirdre said. 'But don't worry. I'll tell you what's happening as soon as I know anything at all, I promise you that.'

Danielle stayed very quiet at first and then she started muttering away to herself while staring into space, or out of the car window.

'Nothing goes right. Always goes wrong. Nothing works. Always trouble, Danielle is always in trouble. Why does she do it? Why can't Danielle behave? Why can't Danielle be good? Why can't Danielle be like a good girl? What is wrong with Danielle? Bad girl! Bad girl!'

'Now come on,' Deirdre said. 'Remember what Angela, Jonathan and I have said before? You are not a bad person, but sometimes your behaviour can be bad.'

'SO IF I'M NOT A BAD PERSON THEN WHY ARE YOU

DUMPING ME BACK IN A SHITTY CHILDREN'S HOME? DO YOU WANT ME TO GET BURNT WITH FAGS AGAIN? OH YES, YOU SAY YOU CARE ABOUT ME AND THEN YOU PUT ME IN THERE! YOU'RE AS BAD AS EVERYONE ELSE, DEIRDRE. FAMILY-AID WORKER? MORE LIKE FAMILY DEMOLITION WORKER.'

'Danielle, it's not the same children's home you stayed in last time, and we would not put you in any place where we thought for one moment you would come to any harm or be unhappy.'

Danielle scowled and started sniffing and snorting very loudly. She refused the offer of a tissue to blow her nose and then moments later a foul stink filled the car.

'Do you need the toilet, Danielle?' Jonathan asked as he opened all the windows to blast out the terrible smell.

'Yes I do,' she said.

'You do?' I repeated, turning around in my seat. 'We're only two minutes from the country park now. Do you think you can hang on?'

'Yes,' she said. 'I can hang on.'

When we arrived at the park and Danielle got out of the car I saw a wet patch on the back of her jeans. It was only quite small and I didn't think it wise to mention it. 'There's a toilet over there,' I pointed. 'You do still need to go, don't you?'

'No,' she said. 'I just went, in the car. Sorry.'

The back door of the car was still open and I looked at the seat Danielle had been sitting on. The fabric was soaked, and I silently ticked myself off. When I'd covered

Danielle's chair at home with the absorbent sheet from the nurse, I had considered doing the back seat of the car too but never did. Now I thought how naive it was of me to think I could get away with that. You could never predict what Danielle might do next; what had I been thinking and why didn't I just cover the seat as a precaution?

'OK, I can clean that up later,' I reassured her, hiding my true reaction. 'Shall we get going?'

Deirdre and Jonathan both gave me a little nod of approval while Danielle gave me a sly, couldn't-care-less look. I could not remember my patience ever being tested this much and I felt nervous and on edge, wondering how this exercise in the open air was going to turn out. This particular country park stretched for miles and was a labyrinth of cycle trails and running paths. People trained for marathons here because it was so vast, and there were so many different routes you could take and open spaces to explore. It could be perfect, but then again anything might happen.

'We'll head to the wooded area, where the picnic tables are,' Deirdre said. 'It's my favourite part.'

'Mine too,' Jonathan said.

'This is weird,' Danielle said, stamping her feet and folding her arms across her chest. 'What are we even doing here? I didn't want to come. This is shit! Everything is shit!'

She kicked a rock on the side of the path and hurt her toe, as she was only wearing a thin pair of canvas shoes.

'For fuck's sake!' she said. 'I hate my life.'

'Come on. Let's get going, and please mind your language,' Jonathan said. 'OK, Danielle?'

She practically snorted her disapproval, but thankfully she began to walk with the three of us towards the woods. Jonathan was a couple of steps in front of me, Danielle and Deirdre. I imagined he wanted to get Danielle away from the car park and pathways as quickly as possible while she was in this mood, as that is where we were more likely to see other members of the public. Clearly, this whole exercise would work better if Danielle could let off steam freely and in private, and Jonathan was quickening his pace.

'Danielle, when we're in the woods you can scream to your heart's content,' Deirdre said. 'Let it all out. It can really help.'

Danielle started marching and breathing heavily, and it seemed like the atmosphere was getting more and more tense with every breath and step we took. Then Danielle began criss-crossing in front of Deirdre and me.

'Careful!' Deirdre said, side-stepping Danielle as nimbly as she could.

Next, Danielle walked in front of me and then suddenly slowed right down. I stood on the back of her heel by accident: it would have been impossible not to collide with her in some way as it seemed she had deliberately blocked my path and given me no room at all.

'DON'T EVER DO THAT AGAIN!' Danielle said, turning round and pointing her finger at me aggressively. Her shoe had come loose and she cursed as she put it back on.

'Please walk alongside me, not in front of me,' I said.

'Don't worry, I will,' she said. 'That's what HE used to do.'

'He?'

'You heard me, that's what HE used to do.'

'He did?'

'Stop quizzing me, Angela! Can't you leave me in peace and quiet for one minute, for pity's sake?'

Danielle balled one hand into a fist and punched it into the palm of her other hand as we continued along the woodland path.

'Can you still go to judo when you are an orphan, living in the children's home?' she asked, looking straight ahead and seemingly talking into the space in front of her. 'Of course you can't! You won't get nothing, Danielle. You're a loser. Lock me up in a children's home and throw away the key. That's all you're good for, Danielle. Or live in a shed, with the mice.'

Danielle's eyes were blazing and bulging and I swapped glances with Deirdre.

'Danielle, why don't you run over to that picnic bench,' Deirdre said, pointing to a spot about twenty or thirty metres ahead of us. 'Shout and scream, run wild and free, get it all off your chest.'

To my surprise Danielle did begin to run ahead towards the bench, but she didn't make a sound, at least not to begin with. Deirdre, Jonathan and I kept a close eye on her.

'I hope this does some good,' Jonathan said. He sounded

tense and anxious and I could tell he was in two minds about how this would work out, just as I was.

'I think it will,' Deirdre said. 'I know it seems like a rather desperate situation, but I think this is better for her – and you and me – than being stuck indoors, waiting for her to blow. If she has a proper blow-out here, in the open air, where she can't harm anyone or herself, maybe she will have a good night's sleep at my house and things will begin to settle down.'

We all watched from a safe and suitable distance as Danielle sat at the picnic bench. I could see she was talking to herself – or was she? We were too far away to hear what she was saying, but from her mannerisms it looked for all the world like Danielle was talking to another person. Of course, there was nobody there, and then suddenly it looked like she was starting a full-blown argument. She was on her feet, waving her arms around, looking agitated and apparently shouting at an imaginary person. A thought struck me. *Is Danielle schizophrenic?*

I thought about the way she sometimes turned and spoke to an apparently empty space in a room, and the way she blamed another, unnamed person for telling her to do things. *She made me do it.* That's what Danielle had said, more than once. I didn't know much about schizophrenia, but I did know that sufferers could hear voices. I wondered if this was what happened to Danielle, and if it explained why she apparently played different versions of herself – versions she didn't seem to have much control over. What was it I had said to Jonathan one time? *It's like she plays different characters when she chooses.* But she wasn't playing, was she? Suddenly a penny dropped. I didn't think she had any choice, because maybe her personality was split, beyond her control?

I wanted to share this thought with Jonathan but it was the wrong time, with Deirdre being there and all three of us needing to keep watch over Danielle. Even though Deirdre and I were close colleagues and friends, I never shared my ideas with her as freely and openly as I did with Jonathan. Also, there is an unwritten understanding that foster carers like Jonathan and me have to stick strictly within our remit. Our job is to care, not diagnose. I knew from experience that even if our opinions or hunches did turn out to be correct, medical experts and other professionals and specialists generally don't welcome such intervention from foster carers. Deirdre, I'm sure, would not have minded me sharing my thoughts, but I wouldn't have expected her to act on what I said, and I instinctively felt it was best not to speculate about such a serious mental health issue. After all, Danielle was under the care of a psychologist. I had to trust that she was in good hands, and that if such a diagnosis were to be made, we'd be told about it, if and when it was appropriate.

I watched closely as Danielle stood bolt upright and began circling the wooden picnic table. Then she bent at her knees and grabbed hold of the attached slatted seat on one side, as if she were trying to lift the whole structure in the air. The table didn't budge and I wasn't surprised; I knew this park well and all the picnic tables, bins and benches had always been concreted deep into the earth or tethered very firmly into the ground with wires and hooks.

The next minute, Danielle threw her head back and let out an almighty howl. It sounded primal, and I thought this was a good thing. Danielle truly was venting her anger, and this was why we had brought her here in the first place. Maybe this was exactly what she needed? I sincerely hoped so.

Moments later, Danielle made another attempt to shift the table. All three of us watched in amazement as she put all her might into it, and somehow managed to slightly shift the wooden legs out of their fixings in the ground.

'Oh God,' Jonathan said, looking at Deirdre, who was gasping in alarm. 'I'd better go over. She'll have that clean out of the ground.'

'Surely not?' I ventured, because it seemed such an impossible task.

Nevertheless, Danielle was having another go, and I had to admit it looked like Jonathan was right. He began to walk quickly towards Danielle, but by the time he reached her she had let out a guttural growl and put everything she had into another attempt at lifting the table out of the earth. Just as Jonathan reached her, she succeeded, up-ending the table with such force that it landed upside down, on its tabletop, with an almighty thud.

Deirdre and I walked over now. Jonathan was picking the table up, and Danielle was standing with her hands on her hips, looking satisfied with her work.

'There. Is that what you wanted?' she seethed.

She looked accusingly at all three of us. We were shocked by the strength she had demonstrated; this picnic bench was not meant to move an inch, let alone be hauled out of the ground and flung upside down.

'How do you feel?' Deirdre asked calmly.

'How do you think I feel? I'm tired, I'm cross and I'M STILL ANGRY. SO THIS WAS A COMPLETE WASTE OF TIME.'

As she shouted a dog walker appeared through the trees in the distance. The lady looked over, no doubt alarmed to hear shouting in what was normally such a quiet and remote spot. Danielle spotted her looking over and stepped a few paces in her direction. Still with her hands on her hips, Danielle shouted at the top of her voice, 'WHAT ARE YOU LOOKING AT, FUCKING NOSY COW?'

'Danielle,' I said, 'please stop shouting. Please don't be rude.'

Deirdre and Jonathan also implored her to stop and we all called our apologies over to the dog walker, but Danielle carried on. Next she made a run in the direction of the woman and began sticking two fingers up to her, with both hands waving furiously in the air.

'WHY DON'T YOU FUCK OFF? WHY DOESN'T EVERY-ONE JUST FUCK OFF AND LEAVE ME ALONE?'

Deirdre, Jonathan and I all made further apologies to the dog walker while we tried to coax Danielle into calming down.

What a mess, I thought. *We brought her here to vent her*

anger and now we're trying to shut her up. You couldn't make it up. We also thought she couldn't do any harm out here, and look what's happened. I'm going to have to phone the park ranger now and offer to fix this table.

'Danielle, have you remembered you are staying at my house tonight?' Deirdre said firmly. 'We need to go now.'

I suspect Danielle may have taken this as a veiled threat that if she didn't stop this unruly behaviour, her overnight stay with Deirdre might be in jeopardy. I say this because Deirdre's words had an instant effect on Danielle. She stopped in her tracks and a softer look crept over her face. It was like she'd felt sunlight on her face; everything about her seemed to soften and lighten up. It was quite remarkable.

'OK, come on,' Danielle said, letting out a sigh and even giving Deirdre a half-hearted smile.

Danielle agreed to link arms with Deirdre and walk back to the car. She did so calmly and without trying to trip anyone up or cause any trouble at all.

'Here you go,' I said when we reached the car, swiftly spreading an old cover on the wet half of the back seat. I did this as discreetly as possible so as not to embarrass Danielle, but it seemed I could do nothing right.

'Oh, look at you, little Miss Organised,' she scoffed sarcastically, although thankfully she got in the car without further ado.

I found myself looking forward to her spending the night at Deirdre's. I was at the end of my tether, though I desperately wished I wasn't, because regardless of the difficulties and upset Danielle had caused, I still wanted to help her turn her life around.

20

'Am I coming back to you?'

Even with Danielle gone for the evening, I still couldn't sleep. The empty house seemed noisier than it ever was when we had several children living with us. It felt like I heard every creak in the pipes, gurgle of water in the immersion tank or whisper of wind on the windowpanes. Scooter had gone with Danielle to Deirdre's house though I imagined I could hear his wheel squeak, and the pad, pad, pad of Danielle's feet on the floorboards above our room as she went to check him, or whatever it was she did when she wandered around at night, switching her light on and off, claiming she was unable to sleep.

Before we went to bed, Jonathan and I had inevitably talked at length about Danielle. I shared my theory about schizophrenia and Jonathan nodded sagely.

'She said to me once that she was two people,' he said. 'I thought it was just one of her nonsense conversations, because she was firing out all sorts of random thoughts, as I recall.'

'When did she say that?'

Jonathan thought long and hard.

'It was after she watched a film with your mum, about a set of twins. I know, it was *The Parent Trap*, that one with Lindsay Lohan. Like I say, I didn't think too much of what she said. And I guess lots of teenagers think that way, when they are trying to find out who they are. Plus, with Danielle being so prone to nonsense talk . . . In hindsight, I wish I'd mentioned it to you.'

'No, you mustn't think like that. We can't possibly ana-lyse every word a child says, and besides, it wouldn't have made much difference. We don't have any power over what mental health care Danielle might receive, do we? Nothing would have changed.'

Jonathan was still picking over his thoughts and recol-lections.

'Danielle did have such erratic behaviour, didn't she? I mean, it was unbelievable how beautifully she could behave with your mum, and how she could suddenly change, seem-ingly at the flick of a switch.'

'Yes, it *was* completely unbelievable,' I said. 'Baffling, really baffling. But maybe this was the reason? Maybe she had more mental health problems than we could have imagined?'

It suddenly struck me as sad – and possibly prophetic – that we were talking about Danielle in the past tense. The placement was not officially over, of course. Nothing was yet decided about how long she would be in the children's home, or whether she ultimately might be able to come back to us. However, I had to admit it seemed increasingly untenable, the more I thought about it. How could we possibly go back to how we were before, especially if she had a serious mental health condition, as I feared she might?

Deirdre collected more of Danielle's belongings the next day, and she explained that the medical assessment was going to be arranged as soon as Danielle was settled in the children's home. In the meantime, Jonathan and I agreed to take care of a young brother and sister whose mother had been sectioned.

'It should only be for a few days,' Nelson said apologetically.

'It's absolutely fine,' I said. 'I'm looking forward to it, we both are. It's not normal for Jonathan and me to have an empty house.'

'Thanks, Angela. You and Jonathan could have been forgiven for wanting a break.'

'Not at all.'

Before he rang off I asked Nelson if he had any details about why the children's mother had been sectioned. As I've said before, I usually wait to be given such information, trusting Social Services to divulge whatever details they see fit, at the appropriate time. In the circumstances, however, I felt I wanted to be as prepared as possible to care for these two youngsters. They were eight and nine; very young, yet old enough to have some understanding of what had happened to their mum.

'She tried to take her own life, and not for the first time,'

Nelson said. 'The children were not present. As far as they are concerned their mum is ill and has to have a short stay in hospital. They're an entertaining pair. I've met them, and I think you'll like them. We're making arrangements for them to live with their father long-term, but he's currently abroad on business.'

Kim and Mikey were indeed a breath of fresh air. They arrived looking like they were coming on holiday, wheeling brightly coloured travel bags and wearing brand-new baseball caps. The vast majority of children who come to us arrive with carrier bags, bin bags or tatty holdalls and rucksacks containing the bare minimum of clothing. Many don't have a toothbrush or a hairbrush, and often their clothes are old and worn out, too small or in need of a good wash. Kim and Mikey, however, had neatly packed bags and even had a toilet bag each, containing all the essentials.

'Have you got a games room?' Mikey asked politely. 'We have, at home.'

He was just a little subdued, as all kids generally are when they first arrive, but he gave me a little smile and I could tell he was a naturally friendly boy.

'We've got loads of games,' I said. 'Shall we have a look?'

'Yes, can we?' Kim said, also giving me a smile. She told me she was eight, 'but I'm only eleven months younger than my brother'.

'Goodness, you're practically twins!'

'Urgh!' Mikey said. 'I'm glad we're not. I wouldn't want to look like a *girl*!'

My mention of twins immediately made me think of Danielle, and the conversation I'd had with Jonathan about her having two lives, or a possible split personality. I couldn't help it. She was on my mind all the time. Danielle's image flashed vividly into my head, and I instantly felt a pang of sadness and fear. Everything about Danielle had become fraught and difficult, I realised. Despite the good moments, for so much of Danielle's time with us it had been like walking on eggshells, which was such a shame.

Looking at Kim and Mikey, who were managing to be as upbeat as possible despite the considerable upheaval they'd just gone through, made me see just how bad things had become with Danielle. Here were two primary-age kids in a strange house, yet making the best of things while their mum was in hospital. This situation was obviously difficult for them, but I could see they were doing their best, and I felt comfortable and optimistic around them already – more than I did on far too many occasions when I was around Danielle. In short, Kim and Mikey were a reminder of normality. Life should not have been as difficult as it had become with Danielle. Jonathan and I had been struggling so much; perhaps too much, and for far too long.

Kim and Mikey scampered after me to explore the games cupboard.

'Can we play this? And this? I love this one. How long are we staying? Can we play ALL of the games?'

'We'll do our best,' I smiled, thinking I'd better phone my mum, as she was the one who had the time and patience to sit and work her way through our considerable collection of board games.

I had a phone call a couple of days later, from Danielle.

'Am I coming back to you?' she asked.

My heart sank. She sounded nasty and accusatory, and she made my mood plummet.

'I don't know, Danielle. I don't know what is happening, I'm afraid. We hope it can work out. We would love to have you back, but of course we would need to know things were going to work well with you in the house again. I guess you need to make a big effort towards coming back, if that's what you want.'

I didn't mention the medical assessment as I had no idea how much, or how little, Danielle knew about this, or what effect it might have on her future with us.

'Do you know what the fucking head of this shitty children's home said to me today? She told me I wasn't allowed to smoke. Who the fuck does she think she is? Fucking nerve of the woman.'

'Wow,' I said. 'I can see that you're not making the effort you need to, to improve your behaviour.'

'I fucking well am! I fucking hate it here! Even *your* house is better than this shithole. The other kids hate me. I've told them all to fuck off and leave me alone.'

'I have to go now, Danielle. I hope you can calm down and I hope you can make the changes you need to make.'

The following morning Nelson called to tell me Kim and Mikey would be leaving the next day. Their father had returned home and all the necessary arrangements had been made for them to move into his house on a permanent basis. The children were very accepting of this, which I was pleased about; their social worker had paid them a visit to talk through the details.

'How have they been?' Nelson asked me.

'Little angels,' I said, wincing a little as I realised I sounded like my mother! 'Honestly, they have been a wonderful breath of fresh air. After all the struggles with Danielle, it's been a pleasure to have a couple of well-behaved kids around. There have been no dramas or arguments. They've had us run ragged, of course, and I can't remember the last time I played so many games and judged so many skipping contests or football and dance challenges, but it has been lovely to have them.'

'I guess they've reminded you why you became a foster carer in the first place,' Nelson said, astutely.

'Yes!' I smiled. 'Restored my faith!'

As soon as I put the phone down I realised I didn't actually mean what I'd just said. I made that remark – 'restored my faith' – as it seemed like a fitting response to Nelson's comment, but the reality was that challenging children, like Danielle, were the reason I devoted my life to being a foster carer. Kids like Kim and Mikey did not need the care Danielle did. They ultimately had their own family members to look after them, and they didn't need specialist care. Danielle was a different kettle of fish entirely. What would happen to her if foster carers like Jonathan and me didn't take her in? She'd be destined to spend her entire childhood in a children's home or one of the specialist units that are dotted around the country. I desperately wanted her to come out of the children's home, and despite the unpleasant phone call I'd had with her, I found myself hoping the doctors would hurry up and do her medical assessments, and that she'd be given the all-clear to come back to us. We could have a fresh start, perhaps with some safeguards in place? That's what I wanted and hoped for.

'It's not the best news, I'm afraid, Angela.'

It was Deirdre on the phone. Days and days had gone by. Danielle had had her medical assessment, and all was not well.

'Danielle is not good, mentally,' Deirdre told me. 'They want to keep her in the children's home, for the time being.'

I hadn't heard from Danielle since she had phoned me in a temper. Deirdre was now making arrangements to collect the rest of Danielle's belongings. I was shocked and upset at the latest turn of events.

'Is this it? Is this . . . the end of the placement, do you think?'

Deirdre told me, in her kind and sensitive way, that she was not sure, and it was not up to her to tell me such a thing.

'I've been liaising with Social Services, of course, and I'm sure Nelson will be in touch with you very shortly, Angela. Please don't for one moment think you have done anything wrong. This is a process we need to go through.'

'Thanks, Deirdre. I understand. Thank you.'

I said goodbye and hung up. I had a lump in my throat and I was really quite stunned at the speed of events. I knew that when Danielle spent the night at Deirdre's before she went into the children's home she was calm and well-behaved. That had given me some hope, but now I was starting to accept that it might not be possible to manage Danielle's mental health with care, love, patience and good-will alone. It was looking increasingly likely that she'd need a level of specialist care Jonathan and I were not equipped to provide. We were highly trained in dealing with disruptive and challenging behaviour, but we are not medics and there was only so much we could safely do. We had to accept this; any decisions about Danielle's future were completely out of our hands, and all we could do was wait for news and instructions.

When Nelson called shortly afterwards, my spirits sank even lower. He explained that Social Services had made a decision on Danielle, and she would not be returning to stay with us, not now, and not ever.

'I understand,' I said. I felt so choked, and my voice was low and heavy.

I did understand, but the news was extremely hard to take. I'd been clinging on to the hope that things could turn around, but now there was no hope left. This was the end of the road, and all I could do was console myself with the fact that Social Services had Danielle's best interests at heart, and I had to trust this was the right decision for her.

Nelson explained that Jonathan and I would need to attend a disruption meeting.

'As you know, a disruption meeting happens when a placement breaks down. The main purpose of it is to establish that all procedures have been carried out correctly.'

'I see.'

'It's nothing to worry about,' Nelson reassured. No doubt he could hear the pain in my voice.

'Thanks,' I said. 'Who else attends the meeting?'

Nelson went through a long list, including Social Services managers, Danielle's psychologist, the head of the children's home, her social worker, Susan, plus Deirdre and one of Deirdre's colleagues. I felt daunted at the prospect of attending this meeting, and I felt very thankful Jonathan would be by my side.

When I told him the news, he gave me a huge bear hug.

'I know how you feel,' he said. 'I feel the same. We've never been in this situation before, have we?'

We hugged in silence for a while and then Jonathan spoke again, holding my head in his hands and looking me in the eye.

'It's important to remember we have not changed and we have done nothing wrong. We have never had to care for a child like Danielle before, and perhaps we never should have. Perhaps these medical assessments should have taken place sooner. Who knows?'

'I think you're right, but it's still hard.'

*

The disruption meeting was arranged very swiftly, and it was an even more daunting experience than I'd feared. It was intimidating to be in a room with so many experts and officials. Twelve people in total were in attendance, and the meeting was conducted with forensic efficiency and attention to detail. Jonathan and I were asked to contribute precise, factual details of Danielle's behaviour, that is all. Our opinion was not asked for, but we didn't expect any more or less.

It was now very obvious to Jonathan and me that the authorities knew a great deal more about Danielle than they had ever shared with us. Though it wasn't stated overtly, we could both see that Danielle had clearly been a top-priority case ever since she entered the care system at the age of five. We'd never heard of so many reports being written, assessments being made and of such a high level of intervention from senior managers and social workers. The physical size of Danielle's bulging case file was alarming, and I was reminded of what Hatty had said to me, many months earlier. *When I first met Danielle, she was described to me by a person in a very senior role at Social Services as one of the most damaged children she had ever come across in her thirty-year career.*

Fortunately, the meeting concluded in a positive way, at least in terms of how Danielle's case had been managed. It was agreed that nobody involved in Danielle's care – myself and Jonathan included – could have acted in a way that would have prevented the breakdown of this placement. This was comforting on a professional level, but devastating in terms of what this meant for Danielle's future. If all of the people in this room could not have done any more, what was going to happen next?

When we left the meeting Jonathan looked ashen white.

'What are you thinking?' I asked.

'What's the future for Danielle now?'

'You just read my mind. That's exactly what I was thinking.'

21

'Will you always keep in touch?'

Susan collected the last of Danielle's things from her room and I gave it a thorough clean, ready for the next child, whoever that might be. I put Scooter's cage on the worktop in the utility room. He'd come back to us after Danielle spent the night at Deirdre's, as he was not allowed in the children's home. When I looked at him scampering around in his wheel, running fast and with so much determination but getting nowhere, I felt a pang of sorrow.

Was that what we had done with Danielle? Had we always been going nowhere, despite all the effort and energy we put in to caring for her, trying to turn her fortunes around?

I tried not to let myself despair, but it was very difficult. I was thinking about Danielle all the time, wondering how she was and what was going to happen next. Once a placement has broken down Social Services have no obligation to keep you informed about what is going on, but Susan had said she would keep us posted nonetheless, and thankfully Danielle had told her social worker she wanted to keep in touch with us. I knew Hatty, Deirdre plus Iris and Kenneth would also let me know if they heard anything, and each time the phone rang my heart leapt.

'Angela, it's Nelson.'

'Hi, Nelson. Is there news about Danielle?'

'Not that I'm aware of, I'm afraid. I was ringing about another child, actually.'

'Oh, of course.'

Nelson asked if we would take in a teenage boy who was waiting to move into supportive lodgings – the halfway house type of accommodation that was very common then, where Social Services placed children aged over sixteen who were ready to leave foster care and live semi-independently. Incidentally, Jonathan and I thought sixteen was far too young to move out of foster care, but nevertheless that was how Social Services did things.

'Gary is sixteen. He's only been in foster care for a couple of months but hasn't settled. We thought he'd be happier with you and Jonathan, if you're willing to have him? I know Danielle has only just left, but it will only be for a few weeks. Gary's supportive lodgings will be available before the end of the month. He's a shy boy, very quiet.'

I couldn't help smiling to myself.

'Let me talk to Jonathan. I'll call you right back.'

Of course we said yes. I think Nelson's call gave us both a boost, in fact.

Even though we'd been reassured by everybody involved that we had not failed with Danielle in any way, it was taking time for us to accept the truth. Jonathan and I were hurting, and we were both feeling quite low and bruised.

Gary moved in the following day. His social worker told me he had not felt at ease with the teenage girls who were also in his last placement, and it wasn't too difficult to see why. Even with Jonathan and me, Gary obviously found it hard to make eye contact, and he was naturally reserved and seemed a little lacking in self-confidence. It couldn't have been easy for a young lad like him to live with teenage girls he didn't know.

I thought back to when I was sixteen, and tried to imagine how I would have felt in Gary's shoes. I wasn't a particularly shy teenager, but nevertheless I understood how big a deal it must be for any young person to live with teenagers of the opposite sex who they don't know. I hoped Gary would feel more at home with us; it seemed a sensible idea from Social Services, to place him with Jonathan and me.

'I'll show you up to your room and let you unpack your things,' I told Gary. 'Take your time. When you're ready, come down and I'll show you what's what around the house. We're having sausage and mash for tea, do you like that?'

'Yes. Thanks.'

To my surprise, Gary appeared in the kitchen just ten minutes later and asked if he could help me prepare the dinner. I thought this must have taken a fair amount of courage on his part, and I was pleased to see him.

'Thanks, Gary. That's very kind. I can't remember the last time I had an offer like that!'

'I love cooking. I want to be a chef, did you know? I'm on a catering course at college.'

Nelson had told me Gary was at college but I didn't know what he was studying.

'Sounds like it's my lucky day,' I said, smiling. 'Good for you. Now then, what would you like to do? Potatoes?'

'Don't mind. I'll do the spuds if you like, and I'm not bad at gravy. I could do onion gravy, if you want?'

'Sounds delicious. Let me get you what you need.'

Gary asked if we could have the radio on while we cooked, and he told me all about college and explained he was also a big music fan. When Jonathan came into the kitchen later he found us both listening to Rihanna's 'Umbrella' as we prepared the food. Gary was telling me about all the different kinds of music he liked, and I was tapping my foot and enjoying the song as I chopped the vegetables.

'Something smells good,' Jonathan said. 'And you're looking happy, Angela.'

'Well, it's not every day I have such a willing helper in the kitchen.'

Jonathan grinned. Welcoming another young person into our home was just what I needed and Jonathan could see that: it was written all over my face.

Gary was no trouble at all. As the week went on he kept his room tidy, helped as much as he could in the kitchen and got himself up and out to college independently. He even cleaned out Scooter's cage, and he knew his way around the washing machine and assumed it was up to him to iron his own shirts.

'I'm very impressed,' I said as I set up the ironing board for him and showed Gary how to use our rather old-fashioned steam iron. I'd been promising myself a new one for a while, but hadn't got round to buying one yet.

'I'm sure you're going to be fine in your new flat. You're very self-sufficient already.'

'Needs must,' Gary muttered shyly, looking at his feet.

'Needs must?'

'Yeah. Er, didn't they tell you why I had to go into foster care?'

I had simply been told there had been a family break-down that had left Gary homeless. He didn't wait for my reply before he elaborated.

'I assumed they would have told you everything. Oh well. What happened was, my dad went on the run, from the police. When he went, I had to learn fast.' He shrugged and walked off to fetch some water for the iron.

'You've done really well!' I called after him, and to my surprise he turned around, looked me in the eye and gave me a rather self-conscious smile and thumbs-up.

During Danielle's second weekend in the children's home Jonathan and I took her out for a meal while Gary was out with a friend. She'd asked to see us, and Social Services were happy for us to arrange the outing.

I was shocked when I saw Danielle, because she reminded me of how she looked when she first arrived at our door. Her weight had crept back up, she had greasy hair, smudged eye make-up and her clothes looked grubby. She didn't smell great either; I recognised the stale whiff of dried urine. I'd been very worried about how she would manage with her wetting problem in the children's home, and now I was even more concerned.

'How are you?' I asked, trying not to show my dismay. Danielle and a member of staff had met me at the entrance door to the children's home while Jonathan parked the car.

'Good. I'm good, Angela. And you know why, don't you? I'm going to live with my dad again. That's good, isn't it?'

'Live . . . with your dad?'

I didn't know what to say. I knew her father was in prison and would be for many more years to come.

'Yes. Well, I mean I'm coming back to live with you and Jonathan. Is that right? And my brother will be there.'

She looked at Jonathan, who was now walking towards us. Her face was filled with confusion.

'No, sweetheart, you're not coming back to live with us,' I said.

'So where did I get that from? She told me that, I'm sure of it. Oh well. Can we go to that place where you can get refills of your salads and ice cream?'

'Hi, Danielle, good to see you!' Jonathan said. He'd only heard the end of the conversation and he added, 'Ah yes, I know you like that restaurant. That's where we thought we'd go. I like it too. Come on, let's get going. I'm starving!'

'Me too! I could eat a horse. I haven't got a brother, have I, Angela?'

Danielle searched my face with her eyes. They were twitching around in her eye sockets a little erratically, and I wondered if she had been given some medication.

'No, Danielle,' I said. 'You haven't got a brother.'

'No, I thought not. Have you, Angela?'

I swapped a glance with Jonathan, who gave me a worried look.

'I did have a brother, but unfortunately he passed away many years ago.'

'Oh. That's sad. But at least you *had* a brother. It's more than I ever had!'

I thought about my brother, Andrew. He had died of cancer when he was just forty-seven years old. Jonathan and I hadn't been fostering for very long when it happened, and it was such a terrible time. It seemed like I'd lost Andrew a lifetime ago, even though it was less than twenty years earlier.

A wave of sadness washed over me. I didn't blame Danielle one bit for the rather insensitive way she spoke to me about my brother; clearly, she was not in the best place mentally. It seemed that Danielle was confused one minute then lucid and normal the next, and Jonathan and I were both alarmed by the state she was in.

As we all got in the car she said, 'You know my judo exam is next Wednesday, don't you? I've asked if I can go and take it, and the children's home said I'm allowed to go. Can you take me please? We just need to check with Susan, that's all.'

I was surprised Danielle had remembered the date,

because to be perfectly honest I'd forgotten myself; the judo exam was the last thing on my mind. She'd missed quite a few sessions because of everything that had gone on recently and it seemed extremely unlikely she'd be able to continue doing judo at the same club, if at all. Nevertheless, I was pleased Danielle wanted to do the exam and I told her I'd do my very best to make it happen for her. This put a big smile on her face and when we arrived at the restaurant she seemed to be in a very good frame of mind.

'I'll get my money's worth,' she joked as she went back for a second and then a third bowl of salad, followed by two ice creams with every topping you could imagine.

As we ate our meal Danielle told us she didn't like any of the other children at the home. It was a fairly small children's home, with less than ten other youngsters in residence.

'They all hate me. They say I get special treatment, but what they don't realise is that I *need* special treatment. I deserve it. I wish these people would understand. It's common sense, honestly!'

It was difficult to know what to say to Danielle. I felt very protective of her and wanted to treat her in the same way I had done when I was her foster carer, but at the same time, as we sat in that restaurant, I found myself consciously acknowledging my role had changed. I was not her foster carer any more. I didn't want to say anything that might make Danielle resent me or make her feel alienated. She was volatile and unpredictable, and I did not want to give her any reason to turn against me. More than anything, I wanted to be a friend and ally now, because I felt that was what she needed me to be.

In the end I just said, rather blandly, 'I think all the children in the home probably deserve special treatment.' She ignored me and told Jonathan she thought he was looking good that day. She did this in a slightly flirtatious way, which both of us immediately picked up on.

'Thank you,' he said, deadpan. 'That's very kind.'

'Right,' I said. 'If we've all finished, shall we have a little stroll down by the river to walk off our food?'

'Can we get an ice cream from the van?'

'No!' Jonathan and I chorused in unison.

'Ha ha, only joking,' Danielle chuckled. 'And you two haven't changed, have you?'

'What d'you mean?'

'You always did say exactly the same thing to me without consulting each other first!'

When we dropped Danielle off later she was still in good spirits, thank goodness.

'See you soon,' she said. 'I can't wait to be back at your house. I can't wait to see Scooter either. Is he still in my bedroom? It will be so good when I move back home.'

'Danielle,' Jonathan said, 'you do know that you won't be living in our house again, don't you?'

'Yes, but I can stay on Wednesday after judo, can't I?'

We both reassured her we'd do our very best to get her to her judo exam, but explained that afterwards she would be spending the night at the children's home.

'OK,' she said sweetly. 'Bye-bye. Thanks for a lovely time! Love you!'

'Love you too,' we found ourselves calling back, again in unison.

We *had* come to love Danielle, and that was why all of this was so painful. We'd had some lovely, special moments while she'd been with us, and Jonathan and I had bonded with her more deeply than I think either of us realised until now. Seeing her little triumphs and witnessing, for example, the wonderful times she spent with my mum, were priceless.

When Jonathan and I got back in the car and drove off without Danielle we looked at each other and shook our heads. Despite her lucid moments, we had to admit her mental health seemed more unstable than ever. Dealing with this was so much tougher than we could ever have imagined. We wondered how we were going to manage Danielle's confused expectations and what would become of her. We had no idea what the future held, but we knew we'd never forget Danielle, come what may.

Social Services readily gave us permission to take Danielle to the judo exam, but unfortunately it turned into a complete fiasco. As we pulled up in the car park of the school hall after collecting her from the children's home, Danielle did a runner, darting back out through the gate and across the road without looking. A man on a bicycle narrowly missed her and Jonathan had to call out an apology as he sprinted after Danielle. He caught up with her less than a hundred metres away: Jonathan was a fast runner, even in his fifties, and Danielle was already out of breath and stopped in her tracks when he reached her.

'Danielle, what on earth are you doing? You could have got hurt.'

She was puffing and panting and very red in the face.

'I thought I was going home. What are you doing, bringing me here? I wouldn't have got in your car if I'd known what you were going to do. I've warned you. I've warned Angela. I deserve better than this. What the hell is going on?'

Jonathan managed to keep her talking as he steered her back to the school car park and encouraged her to climb into the back of our car and buckle her seat belt. The words 'warned Angela' set alarm bells ringing, and Jonathan decided we could not take any chances. She'd made a threat to harm me before, and now it was clear we really could not be certain of what she might do next; her mental state was too unpredictable.

I agreed it was best for everybody if we took Danielle straight back to the children's home, where they were well equipped to deal with a child who might turn violent or need restraining in some way.

'Danielle, you do deserve the very best. I'm going to take you back to the children's home now. That is where you're staying tonight. All your things are there. Angela and I will phone tomorrow and hopefully we can come and see you again very soon. OK?'

'Yes, good. That's OK. I want to see you soon.'

She spoke in a soft voice, nodding and biting her lower lip. I wanted to throw my arms around her and I was silently cursing the terrible past she had had. Nobody should have endured what she had gone through, and I found myself wondering what Danielle would be like had she not been damaged in the way she had.

'Good. We want to see you soon too,' Jonathan told her.

'Yes, we do,' I said emphatically.

'Promise?' she asked.

'We promise.'

'Will you always keep in touch?'

'We will do our very best, Danielle, we can promise you that.'

She waved as she went back into the children's home, and just before she disappeared behind the entrance door she gave us a wonderful smile that lit up her whole face. I'll never forget it.

Epilogue

We kept our promise to Danielle and are still in touch with her today. Sadly, there is not a classic happy ending to this story, but I have come to terms with this and I believe Danielle is now in the best place possible, for her needs.

After just a few weeks in the children's home Danielle's behaviour became so erratic the staff didn't know how to handle her. They tried to encourage her to behave by filling her day with more and more activities, taking her on trips and giving her goals and incentives. Nothing worked and unfortunately the other kids resented Danielle terribly. One night about six or seven boys and girls ran away from the children's home for a few hours, in protest at the way Danielle was being given 'preferential treatment' despite being such a troublemaker. The next day the situation turned critical when Danielle suffered a major blow-up. She flew into a terrible rage and was completely out of control, threatening to harm the other kids and damage property. As a result she was taken to the psychiatric unit of a local hospital, and I found out afterwards that she went in an ambulance, bound in a straightjacket. The thought of Danielle being in that state still brings a tear to my eye to this day.

When Jonathan and I visited her she seemed calm and rather subdued. There was no spark in her eyes; she looked slightly drugged up, although I found out later she hadn't been given any medication at that point.

'I'm sorry about all this trouble,' she said flatly. 'I can't help it. I don't know why I'm like this. It's good to see you. Will you come again? Will you bring me a book to read?'

We assured her we would.

Danielle was kept on a psychiatric ward for six weeks. Hatty and Deirdre both went to see her, which she appreciated. She was great with all of us when we visited, making an effort to chat about this and that and generally being polite and very sweet. I think we all hoped and expected that Danielle would ultimately leave hospital much improved, having been thoroughly assessed, given a diagnosis and prescribed the best drugs or treatment that would help her recover and move on with her life in a positive way.

It didn't turn out like that. Instead, after the six weeks Danielle was transferred to a secure hospital three hours away, where she would be supervised around the clock. We were told she would be staying there 'indefinitely'.

I'll never forget the day Jonathan and I visited her there for the first time. As soon as we stepped through the large glass doors into the spacious reception area we were greeted by a friendly and confident young woman who was wearing a white doctor's coat.

'Who are you here to see?' she asked efficiently.

We gave her Danielle's name and, after looking in her notebook, the woman nodded and said, 'Please, come this way.' As we walked along a corridor another doctor suddenly ran up to us and told us to stop. He said he'd take over from here, and when the young woman walked away the doctor explained that she was actually a patient who had a habit of posing as a member of staff. Jonathan and I were rather embarrassed and laughed nervously, both of us feeling like we'd stepped onto the set of *One Flew Over the Cuckoo's Nest*.

It was upsetting to find that Danielle was much less lucid and even less alert than she had been the last time we saw her, and we were told that the medication she was now on had made her gain weight. She was sitting in a communal lounge, watching daytime TV, and it was difficult to hold a conversation with her as she had one eye on the screen and kept starting sentences she didn't finish. Some of the other patients interrupted too, coming over to tell us things that made no sense.

'Just ignore them,' Danielle said. 'They're off their rockers. I'm the only normal one in here, isn't that right, Pauline?'

Pauline – a woman with purple hair and a ring through her nose – split her sides laughing and tried to give Jonathan a drink of her tea, which was in a child's beaker.

Danielle was eventually diagnosed with a personality disorder – we never knew the details – and she stayed in the same secure hospital until she was almost eighteen. We made the six-hour round trip every month for nearly five years. Danielle's condition hardly seemed to change. She always welcomed us warmly, we chatted about this and that and Danielle usually ended the visit by telling us she loved us, and she couldn't wait to see us next time. She still had problems keeping dry, and she told us this every time we saw her, without fail. Meanwhile, her weight crept up and up.

Occasionally Danielle talked about the past and her time with us. In the beginning we always told her how Scooter was and she said she looked forward to having him back 'when I get my own place'. This never happened: sadly, he died long before Danielle left the hospital.

She often asked after my mum, talking fondly about the films they watched and the board games they played. Sometimes Danielle's memories were very muddled. For instance, she remembered we'd talked about making jam and going to see the Crown Jewels one day, but sometimes she thought we'd already done those things although we never had. On several occasions she told me she would organise the trip to London 'next time I'm in town' or 'when I get time off'.

From the secure hospital Danielle was eventually moved into a supportive lodging home where there were specialist carers and medical staff on duty 24/7. Jonathan and I continued to visit and one day, out of the blue, Danielle told us she had been diagnosed with schizophrenia. I was shocked but not surprised. She said she used to hear voices, and that a woman used to appear, who told her to do things. 'I thought

I was crazy, but I wasn't, was I?' Danielle grinned. 'All this time, Angela, I thought there was something wrong with me, and there wasn't! It was just the schizophrenia causing all the trouble. It wasn't me, after all. I knew it wasn't my fault.'

In all the years, she never discussed her abuse or mentioned her father, or any detail of her life before she went into care at the age of five. It was as if she had deleted that part of her childhood from her memory. She did, however, tell us one very upsetting fact: she confessed that she broke our showerhead so many times because she was using it 'in a sexual way' on herself. 'I'm sorry,' she said. 'I couldn't help it. I was used to the feeling, from when I was a little girl.'

A couple of years ago we found out that Danielle had gone missing from her supportive lodgings, along with a male resident. It turned out they stole a car, booked themselves into a guest house a few hours' drive away, got drunk and ended up being arrested after driving away from a petrol station without paying. Danielle was sectioned after that episode, and she went back into the secure hospital for a while before moving into another fully supervised flat.

We saw her last year. Danielle is twenty-three now and is still under 24/7 supervision, but she is on a much more even keel. She's made many friends in her housing block, has several hobbies and is very chatty and pleasant to be around. Her weight has dropped too, and the medication she is on is working well and causing minimal side effects.

'You did so much for me,' she said at the end of our last visit. 'Thank you for keeping your promise and staying in touch. I don't know what I'd do without you.'

For years I beat myself up about Danielle, and Jonathan doubted himself too. We questioned whether we'd done enough for her and if we could have done anything differently, anything at all that might have changed this outcome. We felt that way right up until she was diagnosed with schizophrenia. That changed our perspective, and Hatty helped enormously in this regard too.

'Angela,' she told me, 'it's an absolute miracle you and Jonathan coped with Danielle for as long as you did. You should be very proud. You gave her a lovely home and a lot of love, in extremely difficult circumstances. You always had a watchful eye and a sympathetic ear, however much Danielle tested you. Even when your personal safety was at risk you still wanted to do all you could. You enhanced Danielle's life, be in no doubt about that. You went above and beyond your duty.'

Hatty's kind words comfort me to this day, but of course I still wish I could have done even more; I'm sure anyone would in my position.

I'm very grateful to have had the opportunity to share Danielle's story. Life is not a fairy tale, and the reality is that fostering is a very tough job with no guarantee of success. Sometimes you have to accept that a 'best outcome' is as much as you can hope for.

Nowadays Danielle phones us often, and she always

ends the conversation by saying, 'I love you both to the moon and back.'

When I hear those words I do believe we did our best, and that she is doing all right, all things considered.